The Super-Awesome & Lucky Owner of This Book Is:

_____

The goal of this book is to help YOU feel empowered, prepared, and excited to grow up! Buckle up and get ready to be the BOSS of your life!

THE AYEEE TO Z ADULTING GUIDE:

HOW TO NAVIGATE ADULTHOOD LIKE A BOSS!

E. Z. GRACE

First Printing: 2024

This book was created with help from Editwright.
Visit editwright.com for more information.

Developmental editing by AJ Jepperson & Andrew Doty
Copy editing by Karen L. Tucker
Book design by Chrissy Holder and Allison Janicki
Cover Design by Chrissy Holder
Illustrations by Chrissy Holder and Allison Janicki
Proofreading by Dana Zwaska
Published by EZ Does It Publications

**EZ
Does
It
Publications**
Learning Made EZ. Growing Made EZ.

For more information about EZ Does It Publications, visit EZGraceAuthor.com.

Typeset in Open Sans and Delicious Handrawn

ISBNs
Paperback: 979-8-9860722-0-3
Hardcover: 979-8-9860722-2-7
E-book: 979-8-9860722-1-0

Library of Congress Control Number
2024913435

BISAC
SEL000000: SELF-HELP / General
YAN051000: YOUNG ADULT NONFICTION / Social Topics / General
YAN029000: YOUNG ADULT NONFICTION / Inspirational & Personal Growth

This book is dedicated with fondness to my mom and dad, B & D. The more I age, the more I appreciate the upbringing you provided me with, filled with love, learning, and laughter. I would not be who I am today without your guidance. Thank you! I love you more than words can express.

This book would have never existed if it were not for the fantastic flock of teenagers I am lucky enough to call my students each year, along with all the intelligent, kind, and compassionate former students I've been lucky to stay in touch with and who've made me so proud! Here's to hoping I will be able to help you long after your time spent in my classroom. Once my student, always my student!

Lastly, this book is dedicated to two certain Super somebodies, who offered to support me in a necessary and crucial way to get this book across the finish line. Your incredibly hard work and drive has always been something I have admired and strived toward. As you said, maybe one day I will learn how to love something that involves more bank account deposits rather than withdrawals! I appreciate you and your support so very much! Love ya!

TABLE OF CONTENTS

INTRODUCTION
Allow me to introduce myself...

WHO AM I?

You might be asking yourself, "Who is the author, and what makes her think she is qualified enough to write a book on adulting?" That is a solid question to ask, and once you finish reading this book, you will understand that asking questions and learning new things is a vital practice that you should continue doing throughout your life.

Now please allow me to enlighten you as to who I am.

Let's start with who I am NOT.

First, I am *not* claiming to be an all-knowing, gold star-winning adult who has everything figured out. I am in my 30s and far from perfect; I will be the first to admit that.

I am *not* a person with fancy degrees in psychology or counseling who is attempting to hide behind titles. If you are reading this book and you work in the education system, don't worry, I will not be making any weird plant-watering, life-affirming metaphors!

I am *not* a mother — at least, not in the natural sense of the term. I have always felt a strong maternal instinct to protect and help those I care about to one degree or another: friends, family, students, strangers, and animals alike!

And last, I am *not* about to write an entire book sugarcoating the *wondrous beauties* of being an adult. I'm going to tell you how it is, plain and simple.

Now, let me tell you who I *am*.

I *am* a person who has college degrees: associate's, bachelor's, and master's degrees, to be more specific. Along with the ridiculous amount of college loan debt that comes with it!

I *am* a person who has been immersed in the education field since my preschool days as either a student, a para-educator, or a teacher. That's a long time, believe me.

I *am* a high school teacher whose students have consistently expressed concerns about how they feel the education system hasn't adequately prepared them for real life. They weren't asking for deep psychological insights or calling upon my years of undergraduate or graduate work for answers. They simply wanted to understand things like insurance, choosing a roommate, and all the other tiny but important aspects of being successful in the adulting world. Each time another student voiced their frustrations about what their schooling hadn't prepared them for, I became more convinced that things needed to change and that I was capable of doing my part and helping to make that change happen!

Lastly, I *am* an educator who works hard to learn, grow, and cultivate a positive classroom environment. One where my students can feel safe to open up and come to me for help to find the tools they need for success, knowing that if I do not know the answer, I will find somebody who does. This is also a trait I carry with me throughout every facet of my life; it's a goody!

The things I am and am not led to the creation of this book you are reading right now. What started as an informative "adulting" packet I created for my students as my graduation present to them has turned into something so much more than I ever expected.

WHO PLAYED A ROLE IN THE CREATION OF THIS BOOK?

This little slice of adulting magic was crafted with care to help you be success-ful and live your best adult life. Many super-cool "grownups" collaborated on providing information regarding the topics in this book. These pearls of wisdom you will soon learn were created using a combination of facts and opinions based on *real*-life experiences.

 What makes this book unique from others in the same genre is the amount of teamwork among high school–aged students, adults of all ages and experiences, and me that went into the creation of this book.

Through many candid conversations over the years, my soon-to-be legal adult pupils opened up to me about the aspects of adulting that gave them anxiety and they wished they knew more about. These conversations resulted in making the topic outline for the book, the content format of the book they felt would be the easiest to learn from, illustration styles, and even the size and style of the book.

And there you have it: Many people played many roles to get this book into your hands!

WHO'S TO BLAME?

One question that has run through my mind continuously throughout this project is: who is to *blame* for this very real and serious predicament so many young people find themselves in?

Is it the family's fault? The education system? The community in which that young person is being raised, or society in general?

Personally, I think it is a bit of a combination of all those factors. How can a child learn from their family if they are struggling themselves? What about the thousands of children in the foster care system?

Assuming that every child will be taught how to be productive members of society from their parents, guardians, family members, etc., fits that old saying about assuming things: "when you assume something, you make an ass out of u and me."

Expecting the community in which kids are raised to properly teach these important lessons is hugely unrealistic on so many levels. Then you have the education system that is controlled and regulated at the federal, state, and local government levels, which really complicates things and makes me think of the expression "too many cooks in the kitchen." Expecting government officials, districts' Boards of Education, teachers, parents, and other stakeholders to come together and agree on public education curriculum requirements is a seemingly impossible hope.

It truly blows my mind how the emphasis on teaching fundamental, critical life skills is so blatantly overlooked time and again. Teachers only have so much time with their students, and we have to stick to our "regularly scheduled programming" to meet what is required of us to do our jobs fully. Veering too far off course, even with your students' best interests in mind, is an all-too-easy way for an educator to land themself in boiling-hot water.

So there you have it: three primary options to aid in answering my initial "blame game" question. Unfortunately, I cannot confidently tell you whose responsibility it is to make sure these lessons are being taught. It's not my place to answer this question for everyone either. The more I ponder the question, the less clear I become on the best response to this dilemma.

In all honesty, I cannot answer it without making some potentially extremely controversial statements. I have chosen to keep those thoughts unpublished and to myself and focus my energies on writing this book and helping out as much as I can. I'm saving that information for my next book!

WHO'S STILL READING THIS INTRODUCTION?

I hope the contents of this book can truly help you live your best life, no matter what demographics you fit into. It upset me when I learned how unprepared so many of my students and their peers felt when entering the adult world. Sure, they can fill out standardized testing bubbles and sing catchy tunes to help remember complicated math theorems, but their knowledge of practical life skills is dangerously lacking.

Most teenagers are painfully aware of this fact and understandably begin to panic as the big 1-8 birthday approaches. To be honest, as a person in my 30s, I still have moments of feeling unprepared. I believe this is a book that can help people of all ages and backgrounds. Through the cultivation of this book, I have learned some handy new things that I have since woven into my own adulting practices.

Find a lesson to learn each time you stumble, then grow from it and move on. Discover a healthy way to cope with tough times. Do not dwell on the things you cannot change; just know it will get better, and you will be just fine. Envision what you want out of this life and then put in the hard work to get there. You got this!

If I have learned one thing about teaching 16- to 18-year-olds, it's that I need to keep things interesting if I want to retain their attention and motivation. Enough rambling about myself — let's get to the goods!

***Please note this information is subject to change depending on your chosen life path and the political climate at the time, among many other factors life likes to throw at us. This is meant to be an informative guide. Please do your own research on these topics to be sure you are making the best decisions for yourself. Adulting is hard and messy at times, but it is beautifully imperfect and packed full of enough opportunities for you to mold it into what you dream up and desire. You WILL make mistakes, you WILL NOT always get your way, and that is okay.

CHEAT SHEET ON HOW TO READ THIS BOOK

Don't worry. This is not the kind of book where I will demand you follow my guidance or be doomed to a life of adulting failure. This book is meant to get your brain working, motivating you to want to learn more and make educated decisions that empower you to live life the way you want.

Allow me to give you some instructions as to how this book is meant to be utilized.

Step one. Pick up this book and start reading it. You are doing great so far! Step two through *infinity*: self-educate, self-advocate, and be open to continually growing and evolving to be the best version of yourself. That's it — TWO easy steps!

I want you, the proud owner of my book, to highlight the information you feel is essential, scribble notes in the margins, and really think about the "pop quiz" questions at the end of each section. Don't let the words "pop quiz" scare you; they are meant to significantly benefit the reader, aka YOU!

I want you to use the provided blank pages to write down the tribulations and trials you've experienced thus far, what lessons you took away, and what moves you made to turn that L into a Lesson.

This book was made to travel with and help its owner throughout all the new chapters of their life. Yes, that was a book pun, and it was intentional; be prepared to unearth comedic gold such as this throughout the entire book. You're welcome.

Seriously, though, I hope you will transform it over time into a book that narrates your personal story.

CONTENT BREAKDOWN

This book was laid out with care and purpose. With that in mind, I want to break down the structure of each chapter for you to be able to get as much out of this book as possible.

 **CHAPTER HEADING AND INTRODUCTION:** This is a brief overview of the topic at the beginning of each chapter.

 **E. Z. DID IT!:** This is a personal anecdote sharing an experience from my life that ties into the subject of the chapter. Use this story to draw your own conclusions and utilize as you see fit for your adulting narrative.

 **WHAT'S IN IT FOR YOU!:** This is what you should expect to take away from the chapter content.

 **POP QUIZ:** Each chapter ends with a pop quiz. These questions will help you make sense of the information you have learned and help you apply that knowledge to your own adulting dreams.

 **NOTE PAGES:** These blank pages are all about YOU! Write anything and everything you want, such as more questions you may have, information that stuck with you, goals and dreams, etc.

THE IMPORTANCE OF SELF-ADVOCACY AND SELF-EDUCATION

Next, I want to point out two fundamental terms you will hear throughout this book. I want to introduce them here properly so you become familiar with them before diving in.

> **Self-Advocacy**: This is the act of representing yourself regarding your needs, wants, rights, and any other topic you deem important.
> - A person who self-advocates is confident speaking out on their behalf and taking control of their own life.

What does self-advocacy look like in you?
- Confident in yourself, not cocky
- Firm and direct, not rude and aggressive
- Comfortable making your own choices and being accountable for the effects that come after your actions
- Respectful to others, understanding that they may also be self-advocating even if what they are fighting for conflicts with your own thoughts
- Being a good listener
- Being comfortable asking questions when you don't understand something
    - ◊ Education is the key to unlocking ignorance!
-  Not being afraid to ask for help when you need it

Self-Education: This is a type of education that one does NOT typically gain from formal schooling and instruction.

- A person who self-educates puts in their own time and effort to learn about a topic as much or as little as they want to.
- Self-educating is a great way to learn and form your own opinions and not be swayed one way or another by someone else's biases.
- How do you learn to self-educate properly?
- Have a place, or several, where you are away from distractions and can focus on learning.
- Come into it with an open mindset and the motivation to control your own educational narrative.
- Understand that what you learn may not always be positive or what you *want* to hear.
    - ◊ Prepare yourself to cope healthily with negative knowledge!
- Find credible, meaningful sources to learn from.
    - ◊ The internet can be a beautiful self-educating tool. Still, it can also be packed full of false information, so take the time to find genuine sites.
    - ◊ Books, articles, sites, etc., that are purely fact-based information.
    - ◊ Books, articles, sites, etc., that are opinion-based or provide consumer reviews.

HOW TO PROPERLY UTILIZE THE INTERNET TO RESEARCH TOPICS

Knowing how to dive into researching different topics on your own is a critical adulting skill, especially when looking into things that involve money, such as researching colleges and scholarships. You have to put in the work to find reputable sources and information. Follow these tips to hone your self-education deep-digging skills.

First things first: Know exactly what it is that you want to research. Start looking into that topic on a broader basis, then figure out what specific aspects you want to look into more closely.

- This is a great time to whip out some paper and make a list to help you keep track of the information you found or want to learn more about.
- Being in a place away from distractions where you can really sit down and focus is a major help as well.

Remember... just because it is on the internet does NOT make it real! Use these pointers to help you determine whether a website is likely legitimate:

- PAY ATTENTION to the site's URL, whether you type it in yourself or click on the site's link from a search engine. Many scammers are purchasing URLs similar to popular domains. One popular scammer trick is to replace *O*s with *0*s (zeros): Amaz0n, G00gle, Yah00, etc.

- Carefully inspect the URL in the address bar. You want to see a site address that has an *S* in it (https://) or has a lock symbol next to it. This doesn't guarantee the site is 100% reliable, but it's on the right track.
- If you are looking at a website that is supposed to be run by a large or well-known organization, head over to their contact page to look for information on their physical locations, phone numbers, and other contact information.
  - ◊ You can also search for the site's specific domain information, such as its age. If you are supposedly on a site for a well-established institution that has been around for a long time, it's highly unlikely that they will have a domain age of only a few years.
- While reading through the information on a site, if you come across a bunch of spelling and grammar errors, that can be a tip-off that it's a scam site.
- If something sounds too good to be true, proceed with caution, especially when it comes to searching for things that you could greatly benefit from, such as scholarships and financial aid options.
- Before entering any personal information into a site, look for its privacy policies. Legitimate websites will be more prone to having their

privacy policies easy to find and understand, especially regarding how they use, collect, store, and protect data.

- Google has a program that you can use to determine the transparency and trustworthiness of a site easily. Just head over to the Google Safe Browsing Transparency Report site and then copy/paste the site's URL into their search bar.

transparencyreport.google.com/safe-browsing/search

BUDGET
LiKE A
BOSS

STACK THAT PAPER
AND HANDLE YOUR BUSINESS...

 Landing your own job and making your own money is a major accomplishment you should be proud of. I am all for a person treating themselves, especially when you accomplish things that you are proud of. Still, there is a difference between treating yourself and being just plain irresponsible. Please enjoy this anecdote about my first experiences earning my own paychecks and my personal debut into the adult financial world, followed by information on how to properly budget and save money in your own life.

E. Z. DID IT!

Admittedly, when I first entered the workforce as a teenager, I often cashed my entire paycheck and then blew it all, poppin' tags at the mall before the ink on my check could even dry. I wanted to wear the *cool* name brands and look good, which, in moderation, I do not see as a bad thing in the least. But the keyword is moderation. Ask me where all those clothes I *had* to have are now? Donated, because I outgrew them by their size or maturity level over the years!

I focus on the fact that my clothes are somewhere being enjoyed by others and the memories I made wearing them, rather than the luxury vacation or the down payment on a large purchase I could have paid for. That is in the past, though; I try not to dwell on things I did *wrong* in my younger years. Instead, I focus on remembering those experiences so I can do better and grow from them. Growth is something a person should be doing their whole life.

Fast-forward a few years to my early 20s: I was starting to make real money, my credit score was bangin', and I was in that young, overly confident mindset thinking that I had everything covered and was being smart with my money and debts — a mindset that you might be in right now.

Budget?? Pssshhhh... I didn't need to budget. I had it all figured out and under control in my head just fine. I now see where that was not the best way to go about managing my personal finances, especially as I took on more adult responsibilities, such as buying a nicer vehicle, paying for my own insurance and medical bills, and so on.

Remember that feeling of receiving mail as a kid? It was so exciting, even if it was just a silly flier! I hate to be the bearer of bad news, but getting mail as an adult is nowhere near as fun. It's bills, bills, and more bills.

It didn't take long for me to start slipping and piling up credit card debt. I knew what bills I had to pay, but one factor I never seemed to remember was precisely when the bills were due. Most of them were due by the 15th of the month, and it had gotten to the point where my first-of-the-month paycheck was not covering it all. So, I started using credit cards to pay smaller bills, automatic bill paying here and there, and telling myself I would pay it off with my second monthly paycheck.

Then life happened. My friends would plan trips or nights out on the town, and there was no way I was going to miss out on that time with my pals regardless of whether I could truly afford it. *Okay then, no biggie*, I thought,

I will charge dinner on my card tonight; I'll get water instead of a fancy drink. Everything is just fine.

And you know what? It was fine at first. Then one dinner out turned into several times a month, or I would splurge on different travel opportunities that arose, telling myself the debt was worth the experience and memories. As you can imagine, it did not take long until I spiraled out of control and was living way beyond my means.

Do you know what is worse than a mailbox full of bills? Having a stranger knock on your door and serve you with a summons from the credit card company who is now suing you.

But WAIT... there's more. It can, in fact, get worse. Did you know that if you do not abide by that court summons, the creditors can begin garnishing wages directly from your paycheck, with no questions or discussion on how much will be taken from your earnings? I wish I did not know the answer to this question so personally because, let me tell you: It. Was. Terrifying.

These companies wanted their money, and they didn't care a single bit about my budget. What was taken from my check was much greater than the minimum account payment I agreed to make when I signed up for that credit card in the first place. My days of living a sparkling-water life on a tap-water budget came to an immediate and abrupt halt!

I had to make some drastic changes to keep my head above the waters of bankruptcy. I canceled my streaming accounts and changed my cell phone and internet plans to the bare minimum — just enough to still continue to do my work and schoolwork. I had to choose between dinners out on the town or buying my animals the necessary supplies to stay happy and healthy. Of course, I chose my pets' well-being over mine; I would never let them suffer the consequences of my immaturity. I ate a lot of generic brand cereal and cheap frozen meals for months.

I would be lying if I said that I didn't have a lot of fun creating my pile of debt. Those times I chose to pick the fun route, all I was thinking about was that specific moment. The instant gratification endorphin high was impossible for me to ignore. I'm sure you know the feeling.

I can tell you with every fiber of my being, that endorphin high was not worth the low point I found myself in after battling with this self-inflicted financial quandary. By the time I realized I was out of control, the fun had ended. Quickly. I was left alone in this giant hole I had made for myself, and I was the only one who could get me out if it.

I am extremely proud to announce that I have gotten myself free of my debts, and my credit score is back to leaning strongly to the right. It took me a little over five years and a lot of personal sacrifices. I turned my "L" into a lesson, and it is a lesson I plan to never ever learn again!

WHAT'S IN IT FOR YOU!

If you read this story and would prefer not to be the main character of your own personal finance horror story, pay attention to the information in this chapter.

Here is some advice: Create your budget BEFORE you are drowning in debt. Even better, make your budget BEFORE you start taking on all the lovely financial responsibilities of adulthood to ensure you can live comfortably on your income. And I mean *your* income; relying on another's income to help with bills and such is a big risk that can leave a person in a very tough spot.

Before you sign that lease or make a large purchase, you should make sure you can actually afford it, not with the help of credit cards, but with your own hard-earned money. Being smart and making yourself a budget first will help you see how much you can spend on different things.

Play around with your budget options and shuffle your money around your potential financial obligations until you find a formula that fits what you want out of life, or at least what you can afford in your life at the time. Maybe you have a long-term dream that will cost more money than you can afford currently. Simply budget a portion of your paycheck that goes toward saving for that goal. Big dreams require a big amount of work and sacrifice.

In this chapter, you will see an example of a budget that I created that works well for me and helps to make sure I am managing my money and bill-paying efficiently. I also included a blank budget template in the back of this book, **Appendix A**, that you can fill out using your own finances and goals. You will also learn about saving money and creating an emergency fund.

While I would have preferred to have been able to share a story of how I budgeted like a boss in this chapter, I had to learn the hard way. I am putting in the work toward boss status and am proud of how far I have come. I hope sharing this story inspires you to crash-land into the adult world like a boss from the very beginning.

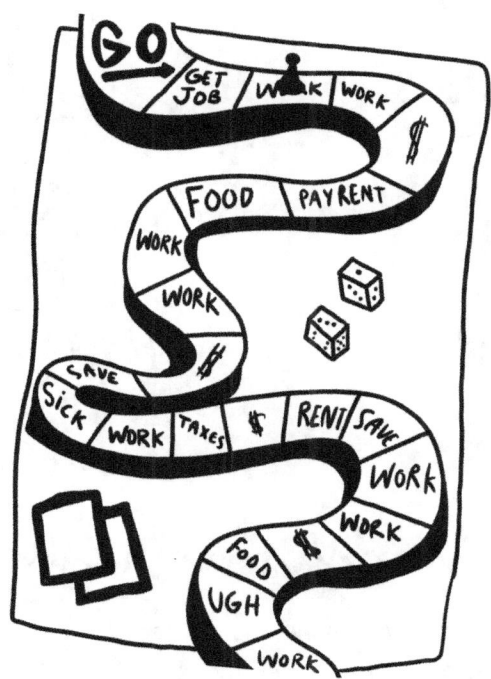

CREATING A BUDGET

A good budget can be your good buddy!

WHAT IS A BUDGET?

A budget is an estimate of the **income** you are bringing in and how much you are spending for a set amount of time, most commonly done on a monthly basis. Making a budget will help you determine how much money you need to set aside to pay for necessities needed to survive and thrive, such as food, water, and shelter, as well as how much money you have left over to spend however you'd like.

SURVIVING VS. THRIVING

CLEAN WATER.   FANCY SMANCY DRINK

Income: A regular source of money that one receives over a specific amount of time from working or through investments.

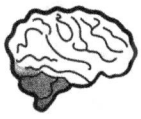

HOW TO MAKE A BUDGET:

- The first step, determine your income. Add up pay stubs and any other monies coming in each month to determine your average monthly income.
  - ◊ Make sure you only include the monthly income you know you will receive each month.
- Next, calculate your expenses. Use bank statements, receipts, and other financial records to determine how much money you need to set aside each month to pay bills.
  - ◊ Be as thorough as possible. A forgotten bill can throw off your whole budget and cause you to overdraw your funds, which is never good.
  - ◊ Also, including the date each bill is due is a great idea and will help keep you from overdrafting on your account.

- Finally, subtract your calculated expenses from your anticipated income. This will tell you how much money you have left over each month.
  - ◊ Be smart when deciding what to do with leftover funds; save some, use some to pay off any debts, and set some aside for your emergency fund and fun money.
  - ◊ Do not forget to include expenses you must pay throughout the year, such as taxes and insurance.
  - ◊ A budget is a "living document." This means you MUST be constantly reviewing and updating it as your income and expenses change over time. Make it a habit to review and revise your budget at least once a year to ensure it still reflects your reality.

E. Z. TIP:

There are many free budgeting apps you can download and use on your phone that will help you keep track of your budget and alert you if you are spending too much. They allow you to easily connect all your accounts, learn where you can save money, and show you where you are spending too much. Make sure you are properly researching any potential budget apps that require you to enter personal account information to ensure it is **safe and secure**.

Safe and Secure: When it comes to your money and personal data, you want to ensure you are working with trustworthy companies. Here are some things to look for BEFORE downloading a new app and linking any kind of personal and financial account to it:

- You want to find a third-party app that major financial institutions have authorized and partnered with. An app that has established relationships with popular service providers is a trustworthy sign.
- Avoid using public Wi-Fi networks when you are doing any type of activity involving your financial information. This will help keep your passwords better protected.
- Before you sign up for a third-party financial app, READ THE FINE PRINT! Yes, it is a big read, but that is where you will learn exactly what that company plans to do with your data.
- Only use apps that provide you with two-factor authentication (2FA) for an added layer of protection. 2FA requires you to not only have the proper login information, but you must also accept a second credential using something that belongs to you.
  ◊ A common example is having a number texted or emailed to you that you have to enter before you can log in to that account.

The following is an example of a simple budget outline I created and use myself. You can also find a ton of free templates and help online to prepare a budget that works best for you. (See **Appendix A**, where you can create your own budget.)

Budget Example			
Total Monthly Income (After Taxes): ≈ $2,400 or ≈ $1,200 per check			
Pay Days: The 15th and the last working day each month			
Monthly Expense:	**Payment Date Due:**	**Amount Due:**	**Income Balance**
Mortgage/Rent	1st of each month	$750.00	$1,650.00
Utilities	7th of each month	$125.00	$1,525.00
Car Payment	15th of each month	$300.00	$1,225.00
Cell Phone	20th of each month	$65.00	$1,160.00
Internet/TV Services	20th of each month	$80.00	$1,080.00
Groceries	As needed	≈$100.00	$980.00
Gas/Vehicle Needs	As needed	≈$75.00	$905.00
Credit Card/Student Loan/Debt Payments	As needed	≈$200.00	$705.00
Pet Care	As needed	≈$70.00	$635.00
Entertainment/Wants	As needed	≈$200.00	$435.00
Savings/ Emergency Savings	10% of each check	$240.00	$195.00
		Bill Total: ≈$2,205.00	**Leftover Funds:** ≈$195.00
Yearly Expenses:	**Payment Due Date:**	**Amount Due:**	
Car Insurance	Every 6 months	$650.00 ($1,300.00 yearly total)	
Homeowners/ Renters Insurance	Every August	$150.00	
Medical Insurance Deductible	Yearly	$750.00	
Personal Property Taxes	Every December	$130.00	
Total Yearly Expenses to Budget For: $2,330			

Utilities: You will need to set up accounts with and make payments to public utility companies to use their services. Common utilities one needs in their home include electricity, water, trash, recycling, natural gas, and sewer.

The types of utilities you need will depend on your area and type of dwelling. You should figure out the utilities before buying or renting a new place.

SAVING MONEY
A surefire way to achieve your dreams!

It is important to do your best to have money saved away for a rainy day. Unexpected events can cost a lot and put you in a major financial bind: car issues, home repairs, medical expenses, etc. It's a bummer, but it is life.

Having a solid amount of money saved can help keep you afloat when something like this occurs. This will help keep you from having to rack up a large amount of credit card or loan debt to pay to solve the problem. Saving money is also very important to help you more easily afford big purchases later in life, such as a newer vehicle or a home.

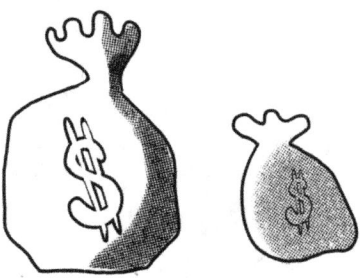

Check with someone in the payroll or human resources (HR) department where you work for a form to fill out that will enable you to split your check as desired. This makes saving MUCH easier! Out of sight, out of mind, and it adds up fast. I wish this were something I had thought about a good ten years before I actually started doing it.

E. Z. TIP:

If your paycheck is **direct-deposited** into an account, you can likely have a small set amount or percentage of each check deposited into a high-interest savings account (which you will learn all about in the Money in the Bank chapter) that is at a bank different from your main bank.

Direct Deposit: The automatic electronic payment from payer to recipient that goes directly into the recipient's account.

EMERGENCY FUND

An emergency fund can help you when 911 cannot!

WHAT IS AN EMERGENCY FUND?

It is an amount of money saved and set aside specifically for unexpected costs. The purpose of an emergency fund is to help prevent you from burning through your savings or going into debt due to insufficient funds.

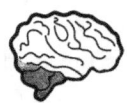

HOW TO CREATE AN EMERGENCY FUND BUDGET:

- Start by reviewing your regular budget to get an idea of how much you are spending each month.
- Thoroughly go over your expense list and take note of anything you can cut out or lower if need be.
    ◊ An example would be switching to a cheaper cell phone plan or canceling your cable or other television streaming services.
- Take your regular budget and separate the expenses into necessary and unnecessary categories. This will help you best determine the expense and funding needs you want to include in your emergency budget.
    ◊ Examples of necessary expense items include food, shelter, transportation, utilities, insurance, and other basic needs.
    ◊ Examples of unnecessary expense items include fast food/ dining out, entertainment, cable, gym memberships, and new clothes.

- Now add up your emergency budget total to see exactly how much money you will need a month to stay afloat in case something happens, such as losing your job.

Nobody wants bad things to fall into their path, but it is going to happen — that's life, and you cannot control everything, no matter how hard you try. What you can control is how prepared you are before a negative situation arises, and if you prepare properly, that will take a lot of worries and stress off your mind instantly.

Keep in mind that building an emergency fund will take work and might be challenging at times. Put away what you can; any amount of money in your emergency savings is better than none!

The following is an example of an emergency budget outline I created that can help you prepare for an emergency BEFORE it happens. Again, you can find free templates and further help online to create the emergency plan of your dreams. (See **Appendix B** to create your own emergency fund budget.)

E. Z. TIP:

Try your hardest to save the amount of money you would need to cover monthly costs for at least six months to best keep yourself out of financial hardship.

Emergency Budget Example

Expense	Normal Amount	Emergency Budget Amount	Amount Saved
Mortgage or Rent	$750.00	$750.00	0
Utilities (Water/Sewer/ Trash/etc.)	$125.00	$125.00	0
Car Payment	$300.00	$300.00	0
Cell Phone	$65.00	$45.00	$20.00
Internet & TV Services	$80.00	$30.00	$50.00
Groceries	≈ $100.00	$50.00	$50.00
Gas, Vehicle, & Transportation Needs	≈ $75.00	$50.00	$25.00
Credit Card, Student Loan, & Debt Payments	≈$200.00	$100.00	$100.00
Pet Care	≈ $70.00	$35.00	$35.00
Entertainment & Wants	≈ $200.00	$50.00	$150.00
Savings & Emergency Savings	$$240.00	$0	$240.00
	Total: $2,205	**Total: $1,535**	**Total: $670**

Notes
Look into refinancing or bimonthly payment options to lower cost.
If possible, call utility companies to discuss payment-lowering options.
Look into refinancing options to lower your payment; just make sure you're not making hard credit inquiries that can damage your credit. (Side note: You will learn more about this in the next chapter, Give Yourself Some Credit.)
Change to a more basic plan with less data, minutes, and add-ons, or get quotes for plans through different carriers.
Cancel cable, cut down on the number of streaming services you are subscribed to, or downgrade your internet service to a slower speed.
Clip coupons, buy generic over big-name brands, resist the urge to buy a bunch of snacks or foods, and stick to the necessities.
Cut down on excessive driving to save money on gas and to put less wear on your vehicle that could result in maintenance needs or repairs. Bike or take public transportation to save money (and the environment!).
Do your best to pay off credit card debts; make lower payments, if need be; look into all of your payment options for your student loans or call a student loan officer to inform them of your financial hardships and have them help you with repayment options.
Clip coupons, check all retail options for sales and lowest prices, cut back on extra toys and treats, or get generic monthly preventatives.
This is the area that is the most feasible to cut way back on; there are tons of free or cost-effective forms of entertainment out there.
If you can afford it, you should continue putting money away to supplement your savings, only use what you need, and do not dip into your savings unless you absolutely have to.

BUDGET LIKE A BOSS POP QUIZ!

Who doesn't love a pop quiz? Especially one where there are no wrong answers?!

Read each question and really take the time to ponder the answers — not how you *THINK* you should answer, but how you *WANT* to answer! Use the blank space below to write down your answers or anything you'd like. It is your book, after all!

E. Z. TIP:

To make this book personal to your life, write down your answers in the area provided and leave yourself some space to revamp your responses as you experience the different twists and turns of your adulting journey.

QUIZ QUESTIONS

1. What are your short-term goals in regard to your financial status? What can you do to achieve those goals?
2. What are your long-term goals in regard to your financial status? What can you do to achieve those goals?
3. What items have you purchased lately that you could have done without and can save money on in the future?
4. What immediate lifestyle changes can you make to open up more options within your budget?
5. When looking at your own budget, what expenses fall into your necessary and unnecessary categories?

Use this space to start planning out your journey to adulting happiness!

_____

_____

_____

_____

_____

_____

_____

_____

_____

_____

_____

_____

_____

_____

_____

_____

_____

_____

_____

_____

_____

_____

_____

_____

_____

_____

_____

_____

_____

_____

_____

_____

_____

_____

_____

_____

_____

_____

_____

_____

_____

_____

_____

_____

_____

_____

_____

_____

_____

_____

_____

_____

_____

_____

_____

_____

_____

GIVE YOURSELF SOME CREDIT

PAY ATTENTION; PLAY THE GAME.
DON'T LET IT PLAY YOU.

 The word *credit* can be a source of pleasure or pain depending on the type of credit you are talking about. Admittedly, I was rather careless with my money for some time. Many adults have gone off the rails a few times, swiping their shiny, new credit card a bit too much. It's safe to say I am not the first one who's experienced a few epic "swipeouts" in my life, and I won't be the last!

I have learned some lessons the hard way, and you undoubtedly will as well. I truly hope you will learn from my stumbles as I have. Read this chapter carefully to educate yourself on this specific topic, but first, please enjoy this anecdote that gives you a little peek into my own tumultuous credit adventure.

E. Z. DID IT

Gather round, all, for I have a credit score-related story to tell. Once upon a time, in my early 20s, I had an *amazing* credit score built up, and I will admit that I got to that point thanks to my mom's guidance. I started listening to what I was told, doing everything right, paying my bills each month, spending the proper credit percentage, and signing up for credit cards with some great upfront rewards.

Keep in mind that the benefits of a high score can be **truly fantastic**, and it was effortless for me to take advantage of all the rewards. Too easy. I was blinded by the magic of the fact that when I charged money to my cards and paid off balances, I could earn "free" rewards such as gift cards, cashback, saving points, statement credits, and more. I didn't realize the ulterior motives behind these "rewards" before the damage was done.

Truly Fantastic Benefits of a High Credit Score: The following are some great benefits that can motivate you to keep your credit score intact:

- Save money on car, home, and loan payments; the higher the credit score, the lower the interest rate.
- Eligible for credit cards with awesome benefits such as cashback or reward points that can be redeemed for goods and services. You may also qualify for travel rewards such as free flight miles, discounted hotel stays, and access to special airport lounges.
- The credit cards you qualify for will have lower interest rates and higher limits.
- Save money on different types of insurance such as home and auto.
- You can make certain purchases and not be required to prepay or put money down for a security deposit, or you will likely get a lowered rate.

It is a system designed to keep the cardholder spending money. I mean, come on, I only had to charge $300 a month, and I would get a $25 gift card to a restaurant of my choice! How can you beat that? Insert face palm here.

It did not take long until I dug myself into a significant hole of debt and could no longer afford to pay off my card balances each month. Only being able to afford the minimum payments on several cards with large balances resulted in an ever-dropping credit score — quite quickly, I might add.

You swiftly realize the importance of having good credit when yours turns horrible. It is a lesson I wish I did not have to learn the hard way, but it's a part of my story, and I have definitely grown from the experience. One of those kinds of lessons where you learn the stove is hot *after* you touch the burner.

It's taken a lot of hard work and years to get my credit back to a good standing point... YEARS! I am still working on it to this day. I just *had* to buy all these things, and because I didn't have the funds in my bank accounts, I paid for them with my credit cards. If you ask me where those things are now, I probably couldn't tell you.

However, I don't dwell on those thoughts for long, as I firmly believe life happens the way it is meant to, and perhaps this short story will keep you from taking the same turbulent credit score journey I did. I chose to use this experience as motivation to do better and be better regarding my personal financial status.

WHAT'S IN IT FOR YOU!

In this chapter, you will learn everything important credit-related, from credit scores to credit cards, the good, the bad, and the annoying. You will understand the importance of credit scores and how this number will follow you throughout your adulting journey, dictating many important opportunities and decisions you will or will not be able to make.

To have and build your credit score, you must have credit cards. In this chapter, you will familiarize yourself with the delicate nature of the relationship between these two entities. Take this knowledge and utilize it to maintain a positive relationship and a high credit score!

CREDIT SCORES

Three little numbers with one BIG meaning!

A credit score is a three-digit number that represents a person's risk or likelihood that they will pay off any debts they owe. Scores range between 300 to 850, and the higher the number, the better offers you will receive, like lower APRs and varying rewards from credit cards or lower interest rates on home and auto loans.

What determines a credit score?

35% Payment History

30% Amounts Owed

15% Length of Credit History

10% Types of Credit

10% New Credit

A poor credit score can cause you to be denied loan options or, if you are eligible for a loan, it will likely have a very high interest rate. Keep in mind interest rate ranges will differ between loan and creditor types. Before you take out a new line of credit or a new loan, research what the current interest rate averages are to determine if you are comfortable with moving forward in the application process.

CREDIT BUREAUS

Your credit scores are determined and reported through three main credit bureaus: TransUnion, Experian, and Equifax. Each of these credit bureaus collects a person's credit-related information and creates a credit report. That report is then made available for creditors and lenders to view and determine if that person is worthy of receiving the loan they need.

Why are there three credit bureaus? What is the point, you ask? Good question! Each bureau uses different algorithms to determine a person's credit score, and they all release separate reports, meaning your credit scores can vary. Ultimately, these credit bureaus generate their own reports to compete for the business of creditors.

WHAT DO THESE RATINGS AND NUMBERS MEAN?

- **Excellent**: When it comes to credit scores, excellent is the best you can get. If you fall in this score range, you will get the best interest rates, loan offers, etc.
- **Good**: If you fall within this range, you should not have many problems qualifying for loans, but your interest rates may still be a bit higher.
- **Fair**: You may qualify for fewer loans if you fall in this range. If you do qualify, expect to pay much higher interest rates.
- **Poor**: If you fall within this range, you are experiencing major credit issues, and you most likely will not qualify for any loans. You have work to do!

Keep in mind that the chart in this book gives you an idea of credit score ranges and options. The bureaus may have different score ranges and may use different terminology to categorize scores (i.e., poor, worst, average, above average, very good, etc.)

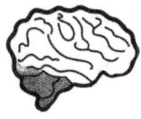

HOW TO BUILD GREAT CREDIT:

- Open the RIGHT credit card accounts! Look for cards tailored specifically for students with NO annual fees or high interest rates.
- ALWAYS make your payments on time!
- Open a couple of different credit cards, use them for smaller purchases such as gas and groceries, and then pay off the entire balance each month.
- Use apps such as Credit Karma or Credit Sesame to monitor your credit score for free. These apps will also give you tips to help you grow your credit. Many credit card companies offer credit monitoring as well.
- Spend and borrow money WITHIN YOUR MEANS! Do NOT spend more than you can pay off within your budget!
- Keep your credit accounts open and in good standing for as long as possible. The longer you have an account in good standing, the more your credit score will benefit.
- Remember, it takes time to build a great score!

HOW TO TANK YOUR CREDIT FAST:

- Missing payments (DO NOT DO IT)!
- Applying for the wrong kinds or too many lines of credit at once.
- Applying for certain lines of credit can result in a hard inquiry that can damage your score temporarily.

- Trying to open several accounts at once can make future lenders believe you are borrowing beyond your means, resulting in a negative hit to your credit score.
- Using too much/all of your available credit. If possible, you need to stick below 30% of the credit limit you are approved for (i.e., if you have a $1,000 credit limit, you should keep your balance under $300).
- Closing credit accounts: **Older accounts in good standing** greatly help your score. You want to keep them open if possible.

Older Accounts in Good Standing: Keeping credit accounts open and in good standing as long as possible will positively impact your credit score, as it shows your length of credit history and your credit age. Future creditors look at this history to analyze your credit behavior and decide whether to open an account with you, what your limit will be, and interest rates.

Keep in mind that "good standing" means making on-time payments and staying well within your limits.

Credit bureaus calculate the average amount of time all your accounts have been open to determine your credit age. When you close an old account in good standing, that will lower your credit age and, in turn, will likely lower your credit score.

Bzzt! Good Standing!

Credit:680

WHAT ARE CREDIT INQUIRIES?

The term "inquiries" has been used a few times over these first couple of chapters. Perhaps you noticed it and were not entirely sure of how they work. Allow me to clarify this for you.

When you apply for a line of credit, or financing, you need to take this information into account, as it may impact your credit score.

Every time you decide to extend your credit, the lender will pull your credit report to evaluate it and determine whether they will approve your application. If your application is approved, they use your credit report information to determine how much they will lend you and what your interest rate will be.

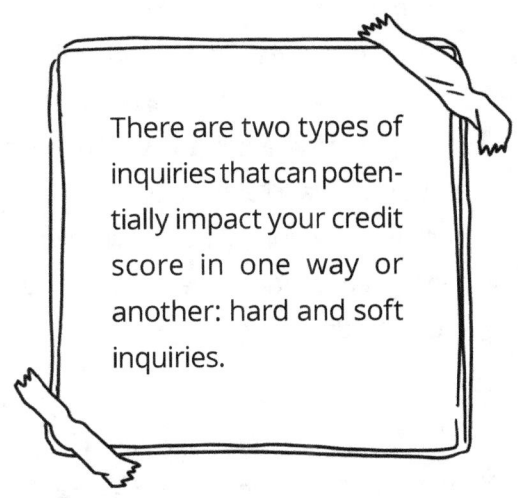

There are two types of inquiries that can potentially impact your credit score in one way or another: hard and soft inquiries.

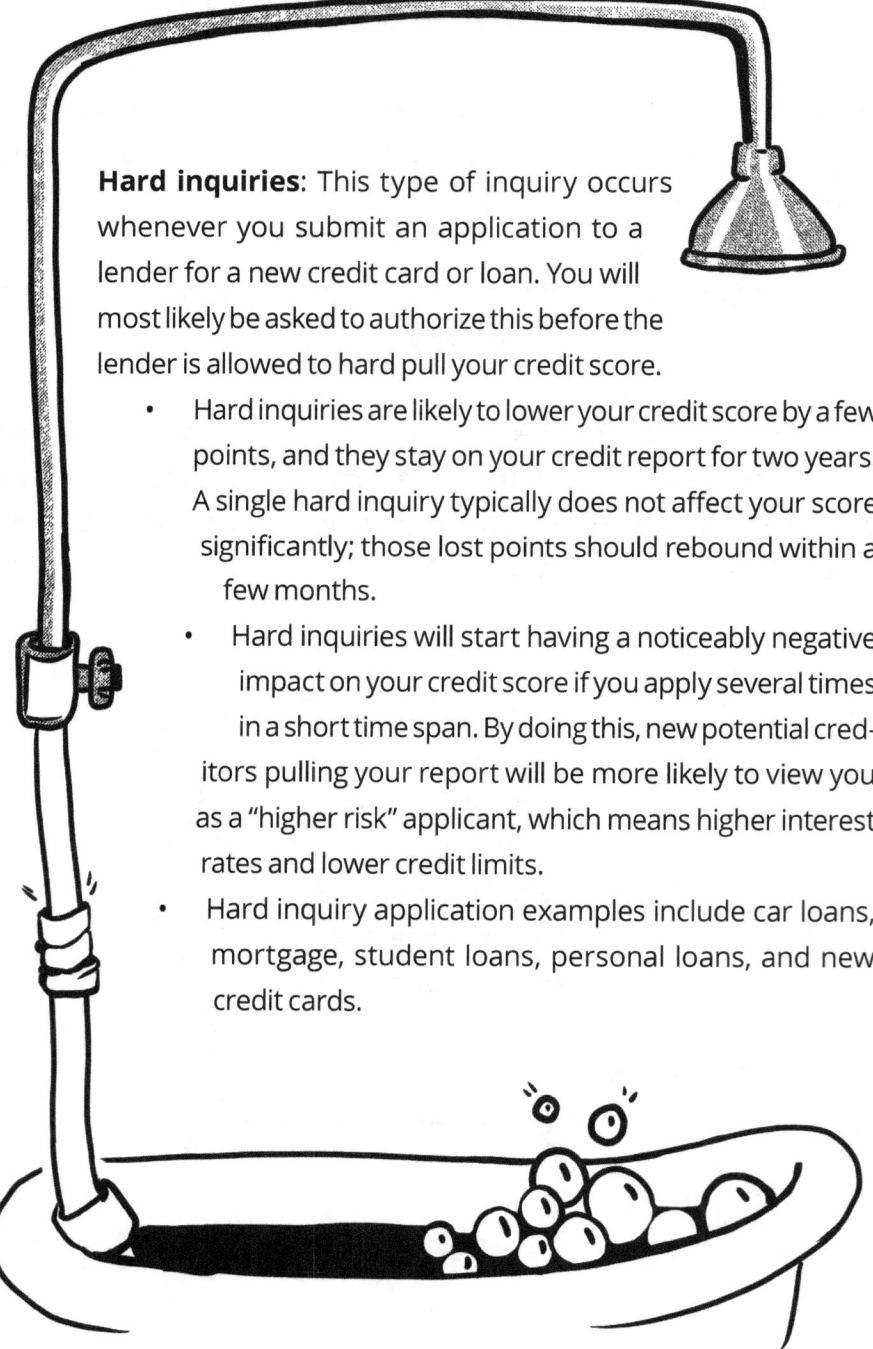

Hard inquiries: This type of inquiry occurs whenever you submit an application to a lender for a new credit card or loan. You will most likely be asked to authorize this before the lender is allowed to hard pull your credit score.

- Hard inquiries are likely to lower your credit score by a few points, and they stay on your credit report for two years. A single hard inquiry typically does not affect your score significantly; those lost points should rebound within a few months.
- Hard inquiries will start having a noticeably negative impact on your credit score if you apply several times in a short time span. By doing this, new potential creditors pulling your report will be more likely to view you as a "higher risk" applicant, which means higher interest rates and lower credit limits.
- Hard inquiry application examples include car loans, mortgage, student loans, personal loans, and new credit cards.

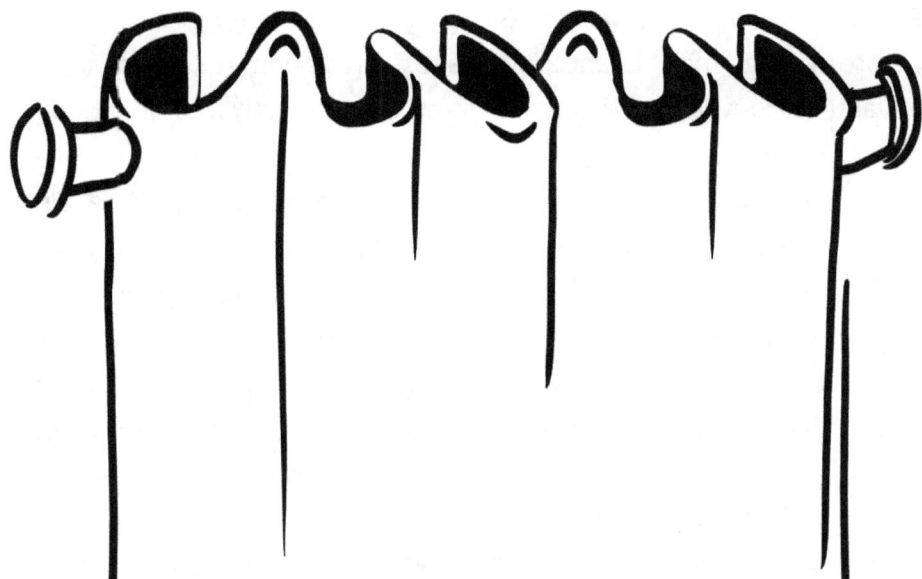

Soft inquiries: This type of inquiry typically happens when your credit report is checked for reasons other than new loan applications. Since your report is being pulled and assessed in a manner that isn't associated with new payments and credit risks, soft inquiries should not affect your credit score.

- Reasons for soft inquiries include having a company pull your credit report to do a background check, credit card companies checking it to see if you qualify for any new offers, insurance companies researching your credit history before giving prequalified quotes, and potential employers doing a background check.

Prequalified or preapproved: Going through the preapproval process before making a major financial purchase such as a home or car has several advantages to it. Doing this will give you an idea of exactly what your budget is going to be.

- Being prequalified for a loan keeps you from having to sweat in a stuffy office while you wait for a financial person to come back and tell you if getting a loan for that amount is even an option. Also, it will help you see what kind of interest rate you will be working with.
- Coming into a major financial purchase already preapproved for a loan amount is a great way to show the sellers that you are serious and more secure. In the home-buying process, this can increase the likelihood of your offer being accepted.
- Keep in mind, getting preapproval usually involves a hard credit check, meaning your score may go down a bit.

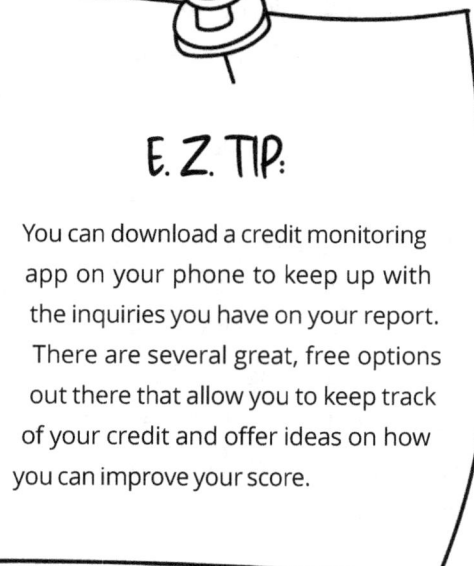

E. Z. TIP:

You can download a credit monitoring app on your phone to keep up with the inquiries you have on your report. There are several great, free options out there that allow you to keep track of your credit and offer ideas on how you can improve your score.

CREDIT CARDS

Your plastic partner or your nemesis? You decide!

PLASTIC PARTNER — NEMESIS

HOW DO CREDIT CARDS WORK?

Every credit card is tied to a credit account with a bank, which will be dependent on who the card is through, such as Visa, MasterCard, American Express, etc. Every time you use that credit card, you borrow money from that bank. As we have already learned, when you borrow money, you will have interest rates and other stipulations, such as making your payments on time and the proper amount you are required to abide by to stay in good financial standing.

CREDIT CARD VOCAB

Available credit: This is the amount of money you have left to spend on that card until you reach your limit.

Annual Percentage Rate (APR): The annual cost of borrowing money using that credit card. The APR is the percentage rate you have to pay on charges that have not been paid off within the grace period.

- Example: Your credit card has an APR of 20%, and you have a balance of $1,000. If you leave that balance on the card and don't incur any fees, it would grow to $1,200 after one year. (In reality, you couldn't leave that balance for a whole year, as you'd need to make minimum payments to keep your account in good standing and avoid fees.) You can avoid interest charges by paying off your card's total statement balance. If you do that, you won't need to pay any interest on purchases you make.

Cash advance: Using a credit card to get cash.
- Cash advances typically have higher APRs and start accruing interest immediately; they're not recommended.

Credit limit: This is the maximum amount that you can spend (borrow) at one time on that particular credit card.

Minimum payment: The minimum amount you need to pay on your credit card by the due date.
- If you don't pay at least this much, the card issuer can charge you a late fee.

PIZZA PIE CHART

Revolving line of credit: A line of credit you can borrow from, up to the limit, as long as the account is open.

Secured credit card: A credit card that requires a security deposit when the cardholder opens the account.

Statement balance: The credit card's balance on your most recent statement closing date.

- By paying this amount in full every billing cycle, you can avoid interest charges on the purchases you make.

Unsecured credit card: A credit card that doesn't require any security deposit from the cardholder.

- Most credit cards are unsecured.

RESPONSIBLE CREDIT CARD USAGE

BEWARE! Credit cards can be dangerous if not used responsibly and land you in **major financial trouble that can have long-lasting effects**. VERY long-lasting effects! If you get into so much debt that you have to **file for bankruptcy**, it will affect your credit for seven or more years. However, credit cards can have many benefits and rewards when used responsibly and can be an excellent tool for building credit.

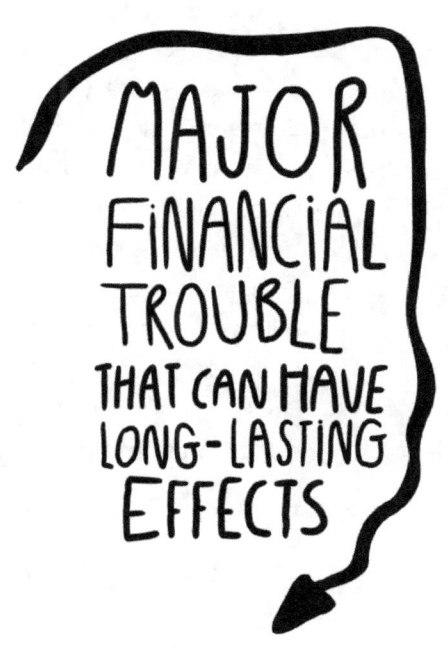

Major Financial Trouble That Can Have Long-Lasting Effects: The following are consequences of having a poor credit score:

- Fewer loan options, with available loans having extremely high interest rates.
- Harder times trying to find a home to live in, whether you want to rent or buy.
- Trouble finding a job, as many employers look at your credit score when running a background check.
  - ◊ This may seem odd, but an employer is likely to see a low credit score and think that you may not be responsible with money management, making you a liability.
- Employers may also check their employees' credit scores after they have been hired. You will need to grant them permission to do so; however, refusing can end in termination.
  - ◊ Company positions involving any kind of financing or accounting will be more prone to not hiring or terminating employees with bad credit scores.
  - ◊ Employers' rights regarding employees', or potential employees', credit scores can differ between states and cities. If you have a lower score, look into these rights for the specific city you want to work in.
- A person with a low score who wants to start a new business will have a significantly more difficult time securing loans and maintaining the cash flow needed to stay successful.
- Some public utility services will require people with poor credit to put down a deposit or have a co-signer before allowing them to sign up for utilities such as electricity and cable.

File for Bankruptcy: You may need to do this if you ever reach a point in your life where your outstanding debts become too much to pay off or you fall too far behind on payments. If it is determined that declaring bankruptcy is your best option, you will need to obtain legal counsel and file. The idea behind taking the bankruptcy path is to help you discharge debts, relieve liabilities, and give you a fresh financial start.

Two most common types of bankruptcy:
- **Chapter 7**: This type is also known as a liquidation bankruptcy; it is the quickest process for filing and resolving debt. The process does not involve you having to file any type of repayment plan, as the bankruptcy trustee will sell off nonexempt items to pay off creditors.
  - ◊ Visit this site to learn more: uscourts.gov/services-forms/ bankruptcy/bankruptcy-basics/chapter-7-bankruptcy-basics
- **Chapter 13**: This type is known as a wager's earn plan. If you have a full-time, regular job, you will develop a repayment plan to pay back a partial or full amount of debt; typically, repayment plans will take place over a three- to five-year time span. Through this type, you may be able to stop the foreclosure process on your home. It is similar to a consolidation loan, where you will make one payment to your Chapter 13 trustee, who will distribute that money to the proper creditors.
  - ◊ Visit this site to learn more: uscourts.gov/services-forms/ bankruptcy/bankruptcy-basics/chapter-13-bankruptcy-basics

Go to the site below to learn more about bankruptcy law, process basics, and other types of bankruptcies.

uscourts.gov/services-forms/bankruptcy/bankruptcy-basics

Keep this in mind! The above links are through the United States Courts, and they provide a good range of general knowledge. You will want to search the court system information for the state you live in for more specific details and requirements.

FOLLOW THESE TIPS FOR RESPONSIBLE CREDIT CARD USAGE:

- Only charge what you can afford.
- Stay well below your credit card spending limit.
- Try keeping a balance on your credit card that you can pay in full each month to avoid interest rate charges piling up.
- Research the credit card BEFORE applying.
  - ◊ Cards will have different APRs. Some have annual fee costs, and others have different rewards/benefits for using them. Make sure you are picking the right card for your situation.
- Review your statement each month to make sure charges are correct.
  - ◊ If there are unknown charges on your bill, contact the credit company immediately, as you could be a victim of identity theft.

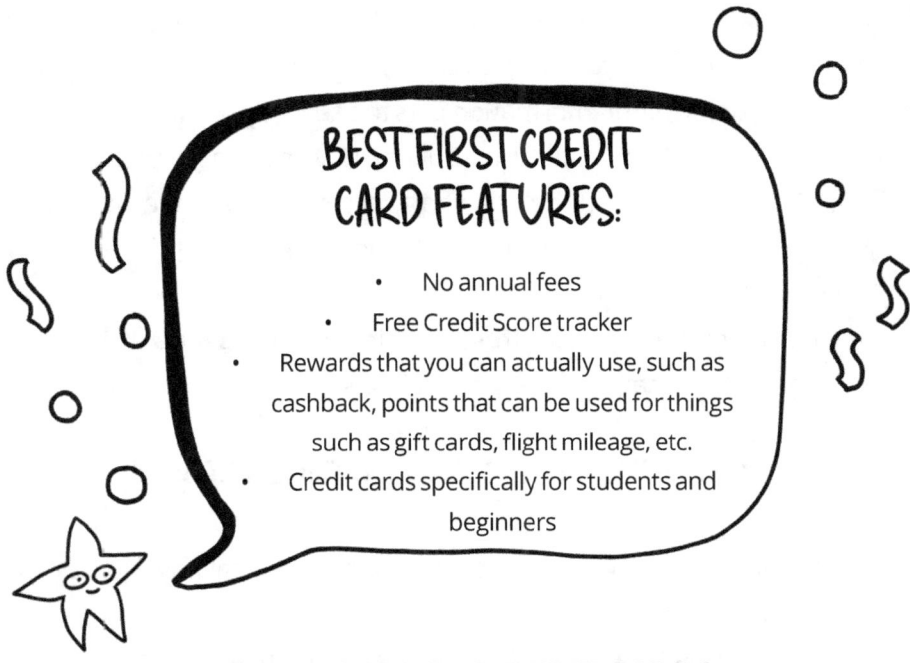

BEST FIRST CREDIT CARD FEATURES:

- No annual fees
- Free Credit Score tracker
- Rewards that you can actually use, such as cashback, points that can be used for things such as gift cards, flight mileage, etc.
- Credit cards specifically for students and beginners

CREDIT CARDS VS. DEBIT CARDS

While credit and debit cards look alike, they are VERY different and must be used accordingly. If you mix up these cards, you could land yourself in some trouble. Keep in mind that "trouble" in regard to this topic typically ends up costing you money.

CREDIT & DEBIT CARD SIMILARITIES:

- Both are tied to a financial account.
- Both can be used to pay for goods and services.
- You use them the same way for transactions.
- They look and feel almost exactly the same.
  - ◊ Make sure you are grabbing the correct card before paying for anything.

◊ Only carry the cards you need to use in case of theft, so you don't have to deal with closing a bunch of different accounts before your information gets too severely hacked.
   + Most financial institutions have options in their apps to suspend the use of any accounts if you feel your data has been stolen. If that is not an option, call the company directly.
• Both can charge **penalty fees** for things such as **overdrafting** your accounts or maxing out spending limits.

CREDIT & DEBIT CARD DIFFERENCES:

• Credit cards are tied to a revolving line of credit that has been issued to you.
• Debit cards are tied to your bank account, meaning you can only spend the amount of money you have in your account.
• Fraudulent charges on credit cards can be flagged and removed so you do not lose any money, making it a more secure payment method than your debit card.
• Fraudulent charges on debit cards come directly from your personal bank account and cannot be flagged and removed.

Penalty Fees: These are fines that are charged to a borrower's account for violating the agreed-upon terms and conditions. The most common penalty fee results from the failure to make on-time payments.

Overdrafting: The act of withdrawing more money from your checking or savings account than you have, resulting in a negative balance. Overdrafting on an account often results in penalty fines.

E. Z. TIP:

Many credit cards have added legal protection, and it is easier to dispute any fraudulent charges or items you charged and never received. Some even offer protection for things like buying plane tickets and vacation expenses that had to be canceled.

Credit cards are easier to freeze and replace in the event it is lost or stolen. Again, credit cards are not directly tied to your personal bank accounts, making them more protected.

Remember! Proper management of a credit card will positively impact your credit score.

GIVE YOURSELF SOME CREDIT POP QUIZ!

Who doesn't love a pop quiz? Especially one where there are no wrong answers?!

Read each question and really take the time to ponder the answers — not how you *THINK* you should answer, but how you *WANT* to answer! Use the blank space below to write down your answers or anything you'd like. It is your book, after all!

QUIZ QUESTIONS

E. Z. TIP:

To make this book personal to your life, write down your answers in the area provided and leave yourself some space to revamp your responses as you experience the different twists and turns of your adulting journey.

1. Did you read the fine print before signing up for your credit card(s)? Do you know whether your credit card has an annual fee or automatically charges you for extra security options unless you choose to opt out?

2. What type of entertainment interests are you into, such as travel, dining, or shopping? Do you have a credit card with reward benefits that best suit your interests, such as travel points, gift cards, or cashback?

3. Are you happy with your current credit score? What can you do to improve your score?

4. Review your most recent credit card statements. Are you maintaining a balance you can quickly and easily pay off? If not, what unnecessary items are you charging to your credit cards that you can cut back on?

5. What financial goals do you have that can only be achieved by having a healthy credit history and score? Make a list of those goals and keep it on hand to remind yourself and hopefully avoid the temptations of buying things you do not need.

Use this space to start planning out your journey to adulting happiness!

_____

_____

_____

_____

_____

_____

_____

_____

_____

_____

_____
_____
_____
_____
_____
_____
_____
_____
_____
_____
_____
_____
_____
_____
_____
_____
_____
_____

Money in the Bank

BE SMART, BE SAFE,
BE SAVING THAT MONEY...

There is a saying that goes: *more money, more problems*. As a firm believer that money cannot buy happiness, I do agree with this statement to an extent. On the flip side of it, though, *no* money can mean more problems too. In this chapter, you will learn about different ways to appropriately manage your finances — everything from banking tips, loan learning, and even retirement. Before we get to the educational part, please enjoy this little tale I withdrew from my own memory bank. (*See what I did there?* Banking humor!)

E. Z. DID IT!

Money management was my archnemesis throughout most of my 20s.

Hi, my name is Erica, and at the beginning of my adulting journey, I cared more about "living life" than saving money. Ironically enough, after years of "living," I started to learn the importance of saving money, especially as I continually grow and take on more responsibilities. It turns out that it's rather challenging to really live the way you want to when you don't have much money *or* savings!

Raise your hand if you have a tiny voice in your brain that you tend to hear only when making financial decisions regarding things you *want* but do not *need*.

"Erica... buy that (insert random material object I probably don't even have anymore)! Why not? You work hard; you deserve to treat yourself. Just buy it!"

That little voice had a lot of influence over me; for most of my 20s, I let that voice persuade me often. It's a fun voice, one that leads you into the land of instant gratification where you temporarily feel happy, keyword being temporarily.

That temporary sense of satisfaction can start to get addictive, making it relatively easy to slide right into a mound of debt that you will struggle to climb out of if you do not make the conscious effort to get a handle on your funds sooner rather than later. This little story is brought to you by a person who chose the latter option.

The truth of the matter is that I have nobody to blame but myself for the financial binds I had gotten myself into; I take full accountability. I could not have had two better parents as role models for saving money and being smart and sensible regarding my personal finance management.

When I ventured out of the nest, I turned a blind eye to those lessons. Why? Because I wanted to have fun in the way I thought I *needed* to! Let me tell you: I did, in fact, have a lot of fun. I can't even lie about that. As a young adult, I went through this period when I felt I knew what was best and right for myself, and nobody could tell me anything different.

What I really ended up doing was spending well over my means. I constantly told myself I would work hard, and next month, I would stick to a strict budget... which is hard to do when your budget is imaginary. I am proud to report that I have since gotten a handle on this situation and have turned this L into a Lesson, albeit an expensive one!

The *real* lesson I learned is that I do *not* require any money at all to still have a ton of fun experiences and make lifelong memories with my friends. It truly is not about the money; it is about the people you love and surround yourself with.

We live in a society that preaches the importance of having wealth, especially as a status symbol. However, if you really take a step back and observe people with seemingly unlimited funds, you will likely notice that they are not as happy and carefree as you would imagine. Again, I will reflect upon the saying, *more money, more problems*. It keeps me grounded and reminds me of what truly matters at the end of the day — my happiness.

WHAT'S IN IT FOR YOU!

Perhaps you might go through that phase yourself. And you know what? That is okay; adulting is all about trial and error and finding your place in this crazy world we live in. Ultimately, you will make the choices that you want, and it is up to you to decide what advice you choose to listen to. You are also going to be the one who will have to take ownership of your choices and deal with the resulting consequences. Taking responsibility for your actions can be a major drag at times, but look at it as a lesson and an opportunity for growth.

Learning how to better understand loans, proper banking, and interest rates isn't necessarily the most exciting adventure. The rest of this chapter may be a bit bland and perhaps even overwhelming, but it is something everyone should learn and understand in order to make *smart* choices.

I suggest you take your time reading and absorbing this information. Go slow, take breaks, and skip around to other chapters of the book if you want to — a bit of a "choose your own adventure" type of guide, if you will. After all, it is *your* life and *your* book to handle as you see fit!

I will end this section with another mantra that often runs through my mind: *money does not buy happiness*. I can't express how true this saying is, and I hope you learn that lesson quicker than I did by reading this book!

INTEREST RATES

Sadly, they are not as interesting as they sound!

WHAT IS AN INTEREST RATE?

An interest rate is a specified percentage that is added to the amount of money being borrowed or saved. Interest rates can be good or bad.

Good interest: This is the interest you earn on the money you are saving.
- Different banks and account types will offer you different interest rates for saving your money there.
- Keep in mind that this is not a significant sum by any means. The average interest rate of a savings account is 0.05%.
- There are **high-yield accounts** you can save your money in that offer higher interest rates. Just make sure you understand the account requirements and details, such as any deposit requirements, balance minimums, fees, interest rates, and if there are any time restrictions on when you can access your money.

Bad interest: This is the interest rate that you are charged by the lender for borrowing money. What can be bad about it is high interest rates. This is where having a good credit score is so important.
- **E. Z. example:** If you purchase a home costing $150,000, and a lender agrees to loan you the funds with a fixed interest rate of 7% on a 30 year loan, you will end up paying a total of $465,000!
- Yearly interest amount: $150,000 x 7% = $10,500
- Total interest for a 30 year loan: $10,500 x 30 = $315,000

- Total ACTUAL cost if you make the minimum payment on-time for 30 years: $150,000 + $315,000 = $465,000

High-Yield Accounts: This type of account is similar to a standard savings account but pays a higher annual percentage yield (APY) on your money. This type of account will offer you safety through federal insurance and will better protect your principal.

- Before opening an account, learn the deposit and balance requirements, APY, any stipulations regarding withdrawals, and potential account fees.
- The national average APY for a regular savings account is 0.06%, while the average yield for a high-yield account is around 1.50% — over 20 times higher!
  ◊ Example: You have $2,500 that you want to deposit into some kind of savings account, and you want to know what your yield options could be between regular savings and high-yield accounts.
    + A regular savings account with a 0.06% APY will earn about $1.50 over a year.
    + A high-yield account with a 1.50% APY will earn about $37.50 in a year.
- Please note that interest rates can fluctuate at any time, so keep a close eye on your high-yield account to ensure you are getting the most out of it. Many financial institutions will offer a high APY upfront and decrease it over time.

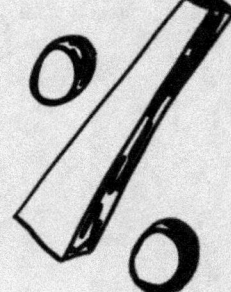

One way to avoid paying for all of the added interest is by making payments more frequently or larger than the bare minimum. Keep this in mind to help you make the right financial choices for your situation.

Remember! The *final* price you decide to pay on any purchase requiring you to take out a loan and pay interest is not the actual amount you will pay. Even if you make all your payments on time and in full, you will still be paying quite a bit more than that initial *final* purchase price, so make sure you keep that in mind.

BANKING FORMS & CHECKS

It's really hard to make forms sound fun, but I will try... YAY forms!!!

Account types: The two main bank account types you need to be concerned about as a young adult are checking and savings accounts.

- **Checking account:** This is the account that most people will deposit their paychecks into and use for day-to-day spending. This account type comes with a debit card and checks.
  - ◊ **REMEMBER:** You can only spend the amount of money you have in your account.
- **Savings account:** A savings account is an interest-bearing account used to hold money for short-term or long-term goals or emergencies. You can add to this account at any time, but **certain types of withdrawals** may be limited.
  - ◊ It is typically not as easy to access money in savings accounts, as they are classified as nontransaction account types. They are a great account option to help you avoid spending temptations.
  - ◊ Be sure to research bank options to find an account type that fits your needs.

Certain Types of Withdrawals: Depending on the particular financial institution, there may be withdrawal regulations such as making online transfers between either different accounts or different institutions, overdraft transfers to a checking account, outgoing wire transfers, and automatic transfers for bill payments or payment services.

Banking slip preparation: Let's talk briefly about withdrawal and deposit slips.

- **Withdrawal slip:** Fill out this slip to give to the teller when you want to withdraw money from one of your bank accounts.
- **Deposit slip:** Fill this slip out to give to the teller along with the money you want to deposit into your account.

Fill it out right: You MUST have these slips properly filled out to deposit or receive funds. Make sure you also have **acceptable forms of ID** with you, or you will likely be turned away.

Acceptable Forms of ID: Personal identification options you can use when opening an account: government-issued driver's license, birth certificate, passport, or social security card. Note that you will likely need the original documents, not photocopies, to qualify.

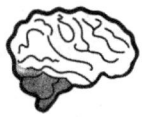

Use the following examples to learn how to fill out banking slips correctly.

HOW TO FILL OUT A WITHDRAWAL SLIP:

- Fill out the required information: name, date, account number, etc.
- List the amount of money you would like to withdraw from your account. Remember, you cannot take out what you do not have.
- Sign slip and give it to the bank teller along with your ID.

WITHDRAWAL SLIP

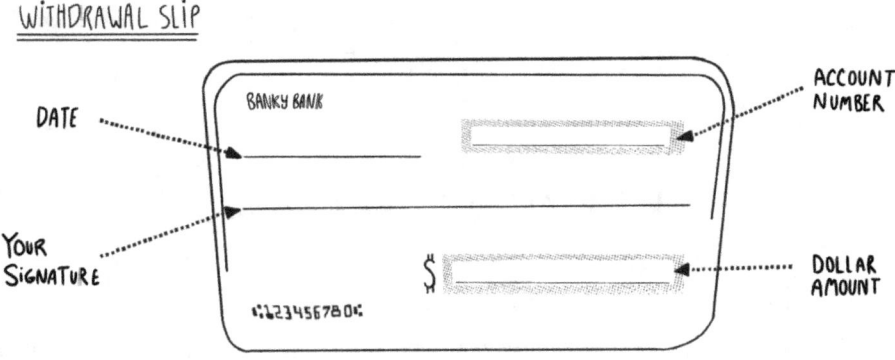

HOW TO FILL OUT A DEPOSIT SLIP:

- Fill out the required information: name, date, account number, etc.
- List the amount of money you want to deposit. Add the cash and checks separately to determine your subtotal.
- If you are depositing checks and want cash back, enter that amount in the "Less Cash" box and then subtract that amount from the sub-total to get the total amount you want to deposit.

CHECKING DEPOSIT SLIP

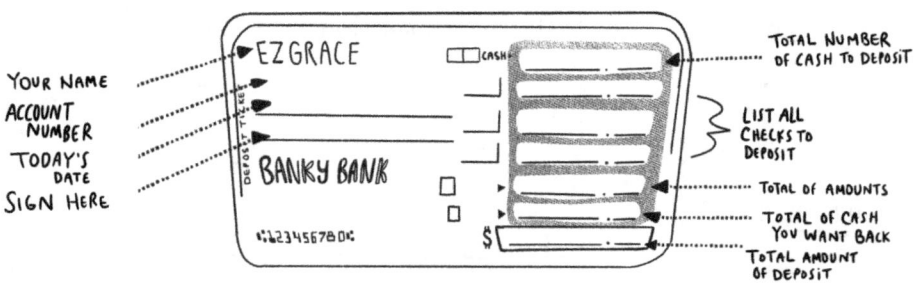

HOW TO FILL OUT A CHECK:

- Enter the date at the top of the check.
- Write the name of the company or person you are paying in the "**Pay to the Order of**" line.
- At the end of the "**Pay to the Order of**" line, write the number amount of the check inside the box (for example, 22.30).
- On the "**Dollars**" line, write out the monetary number amount of the check.

◊ This confirms the number amount you wrote in the box; for example, Twenty-Two and 30/100. Note that you should write the cents as a numerical fraction.

◊ If there is blank space left after you write in the amount, draw a line out to the end, stopping before the word "Dollars." This way, no one can add to the amount and easily scam you.

+ For example,

Twenty-Two and 30/100----------------------Dollars

• Write your signature on the line at the lower-right corner of your check.

◊ See **Appendix D** to learn the cursive alphabet so you can fine-tune your adult signature skills, as you will use them a lot in life.

• In the "Memo" section, bottom-left corner, write what the check is for.

◊ For example, "Rent Payment for April."

EZ GRACE
123 MAIN St.
ANYTOWN, USA 11111

DATE Jan. 1, 2023

PAY to THE
ORDER OF SUPER TASTY CANDY SHOP $ 27.15

TWENTY-SEVEN AND 15/100 DOLLARS

MEMO Candy for friends! SIGNATURE EZ Grace

I:123456789I: 1001001234II• 0123

LOANS
A monetary advance that can leave you at a disadvantage!

WHAT IS A LOAN?

A loan is when you receive money from a friend, bank, or a financial institution in exchange for future repayment of the principal plus interest. The principal is the amount you borrowed, and the interest is the amount you are charged for receiving the loan.

THE THREE COMPONENTS OF A LOAN:

The interest component: The interest component or interest rate is the lender's charge for using their money. The interest rate is usually a small percentage of the amount loaned.

- There are two different types of interest rates: fixed or variable (aka adjustable).
    - ◊ **Fixed rate:** The interest rate is fixed and will NOT change for the life of the loan.
    - ◊ **Variable rate:** The interest rate can change over time. The rate is usually based on the standard market rate at the time.

The security component: All loans are either secured or unsecured. This refers to whether you are putting up assets, often referred to as collateral, to guarantee your loan.

- **Secured loans:** This type of loan means you have guaranteed the lender will be repaid one way or another by giving them a claim on something you own, which is called collateral.

◊ If the loan goes unpaid, the lender can seize the **collateral** you put up to recoup their investment.

- **Unsecured loans:** This type of loan does not require collateral from the borrower. The bank, therefore, has no protection if the loan goes unpaid. Unsecured loans almost always have higher interest rates than secured loans.

The term component: The term is the length of time you have to pay the loan back. Longer terms tend to have higher interest rates.

> **Collateral:** This is when you offer something to a lender to secure a payment, knowing that if you default on your payments, that asset will be forfeited.
>
> - Common examples include taking out a loan when purchasing a vehicle or a home. These items can be repossessed if you do not honor your loan repayment requirements.

LOAN EXAMPLE

Meet Pat. Pat decided to take out a $10,000 secured loan with an interest rate of 8.25% and a 10-year term. Because this is a secured loan, Pat uses their 2014 Ford Mustang as collateral. Pat's loan breaks down as follows:

Loan balance: $10,000
Loan interest rate: 8.25%
Monthly payment: $122.65
Number of payments: 120
Total payment: $14,718.32
Total interest paid: $4,718.32

The minimum monthly payment that Pat needs to make to complete their loan within the 10-year term is $122.65. After 120 payments of $122.65, Pat will have paid off the entire loan and $4,718.49 in interest.

Keep in mind that Pat can always increase their monthly payments. This will shorten the loan's term and result in less interest paid. For instance, if Pat decides to pay $250 each month, their repayment plan breaks down as follows:

Loan balance: $10,000
Loan interest rate: 8.25%
Monthly payment: $249.71
Number of payments: 47
Total payment: $11,736.37
Total interest paid: $1,736.37

By upping their monthly payment, Pat shortens the term of the loan to 47 months, or just under four years. Pat also reduces the total interest they will pay to $1,736.37.

Let's say that instead of upping their monthly payments, Pat skips a few. In fact, let's say Pat decides to stop paying the loan altogether. That's *bad* news for Pat. Because this is a secure loan, Pat will likely be kissing their Mustang goodbye.

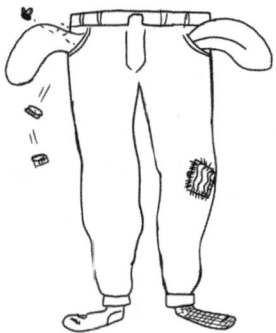

If you ever consider taking out a loan, pay special attention to the basic terms to anticipate how much you'll pay and how long you'll be in debt. Strive to be the Pat who makes extra payments and saves interest money, not the Pat who decides to break the loan agreement and suffers major consequences because of the choice they made.

COMMON LOAN TYPES

Payday loans (AVOID if possible): A short-term, high-cost loan that typically needs to be repaid by your next payday. Loan amount, fees, and repayment time vary depending on your location. Suitable for emergency cash when there are no other options.

Title loans (AVOID if possible): A loan you can take out if you own your vehicle. You can typically borrow between 25% and 50% of your vehicle's value. Usually needs to be repaid within 15 to 30 days. This type of loan tends to have very high annual percentage rates, and if not paid off in time, your car can get repossessed.

Payday alternative loans: A short-term loan offered by some federal credit unions tends to be more affordable than a payday loan. Better lower interest rate options and longer repayment periods.

Home equity loans: A secured loan where your home is used as collateral to borrow a lump sum of money. The equity amount you can borrow is figured out by taking the difference between the market value of your house and the amount you still owe.

- These are a good alternative to personal loans, but your home can be **foreclosed** on if you default on payments.

Credit card cash advances: A short-term loan that you can borrow against your credit card balance. Not available with every card. Watch out for high interest rates and added fees.

Foreclosure: This happens when you fall behind or skip out on your mortgage payments to the point that the lender repossesses and resells the home. As previously mentioned, when you agree to purchase a home and take out a loan, you use the property as collateral.

Keep in mind: If you are looking into purchasing a home that has been foreclosed on, it is highly likely that the home will need a lot of repairs, which can quickly add up. Many people will stop any kind of maintenance or home care once they realize they are losing their house.

RETIREMENT

Time flies! Start saving when you are young so you can enjoy the sweet life when you're old!

I know this seems like a weird topic to discuss, especially if you are a young whippersnapper just starting your adulting life, but time really does fly by. If you want to retire at a decent age and enjoy your *golden years*, it is never too early to start planning and saving.

THINGS TO THINK ABOUT:

- At what age would you like to be retired, and where would you like to be financially at retirement?
- Do you have a 401(k) or any other type of account through your employer? If yes, how much of your pay is deducted and put into this account? And does your employer match your contribution?
- What type of retirement account is the best option for your goals?
- What age do you have to be to withdraw money from your account? What is the penalty fee for the early withdrawal of funds?

- Are you paying taxes on the money when you put it into an account or when it is time to withdraw?
- Do you like free money? If so, research your options and invest early to take full advantage of your retirement account(s).

BANKING VOCAB:

APR: Annual percentage rate. The amount of interest you gain from keeping money in an account in a year, not including compound interest. In the context of a loan, the APR represents the cost of borrowing money.

APY: Annual percentage yield. The amount of interest you gain from keeping money in an account in a year, including compound interest.

Certificate of deposit: Commonly known as a CD, this is an account into which you deposit a sum of money and agree to keep it there for a specified length of time.
- This type of account typically pays higher interest rates than standard savings and checking accounts.

Commercial bank: These banks work with businesses.

Compound interest: Interest that applies to the original deposit and any newly earned interest.
- For example, if you put $100 in an account that earns compound interest at 5% a year, in the next year, you will earn 5% on $105. Non-compounding interest would continue to earn 5% on $100.

Credit unions: These banks work with specific fields, such as military and teachers; they require a membership.

FDIC: The Federal Deposit Insurance Corp. A government-run organization that insures customers' bank deposits up to $250,000 if the bank fails.

Internet bank: These banks are similar to retail banks, but everything is done online.

- This is a newer bank type; do your research before committing to one.

Overdraft fee: A fee incurred when your checking account doesn't have enough funds to cover a requested payment. The financial institution will pay what your account lacks, after which your account may have a negative balance.

Retail bank: These banks offer products to, and work with, individuals.

Returned item fee: A bounced-check fee charged to the person trying to deposit the check. It can be charged if insufficient funds are in the check writer's account or if the account is closed.

Routing number: A nine-digit number that identifies your financial institution, typically found in the lower left part of the check.

RETIREMENT ACCOUNT VOCAB:

401(k): This is an employer-sponsored retirement account option that is offered by for-profit organizations, where money in the account is grown through investments. You can invest a portion of your salary (pretaxed) into this account by having it automatically deducted from your check.

- Make sure you check the specific details of what your employer offers to match and what investment opportunities are available so that you can take full advantage of this type of account.

403(b): This account is similar to the 401(k). It is offered to employees of nonprofit and tax-exempt organizations, such as public school and government employees. This account typically does not have as many investment opportunities, and employers are less likely to match contributions.

- **Note:** Both the 401(k) and 403(b) accounts have limits as to how much you can contribute each year. Typically, these accounts have early withdrawal or tax penalty fees. They may also offer a tax-free Roth option. Make sure you figure out when your account will be taxed — immediately or when you reach retirement age.

IRA (Individual Retirement Account): This is a tax-advantaged retirement account you can open on your own. It's the better option for those who are self-employed. The money contributed to this account type is not taxed when it is first deposited, which can be beneficial when you withdraw at retirement if you are in a lower tax bracket.

Rollover IRA: This account is good for people who have switched jobs and need an option to roll over the money from employer-sponsored accounts (401(k), 403(b), etc.).

Roth IRA: This account is similar to the IRA. The difference is you have already paid taxes on the money you put into this account, meaning tax-free growth and retirement withdrawal.

- **Note:** IRAs are a great retirement saving option to supplement your other retirement accounts.

MONEY IN THE BANK POP QUIZ!

Who doesn't love a pop quiz? Especially one where there are no wrong answers?!

Read each question and really take the time to ponder the answers — not how you *THINK* you should answer, but how you *WANT* to answer! Use the blank space below to write down your answers or anything you'd like. It is your book, after all!

E. Z. TIP:

To make this book personal to your life, write down your answers in the area provided and leave yourself some space to revamp your responses as you experience the different twists and turns of your adulting journey.

QUIZ QUESTIONS

1. What are the "big-ticket items" you want, such as a home, car, etc.? Will you need to take out a loan to afford these?

2. Have you researched all the different loan options you qualify for? Are you absolutely positive you have loans with the best interest rates and payment amounts?

3. If you have multiple loans, have you looked into options to consolidate the loans to save money on interest and payments?

4. What types of accounts do you currently have? Are you satisfied with your current accounts, or is there an account type that better suits your financial needs?

5. Have you reviewed the benefits your bank offers recently? Does your current bank provide you with everything you want? (Different banks

offer different benefits, so make sure you find the right fit for your needs.)

Use this space to start planning out your journey to adulting happiness!

_____

_____

_____

_____

_____

_____

_____

_____

_____

_____

_____

_____

_____

_____

_____

_____

_____

_____

_____

_____

_____

_____

_____

_____

_____

_____

_____

_____

_____

_____

_____

_____

_____

Taxes are taxing

YOU DON'T HAVE TO LIKE IT;
YOU DO HAVE TO DO IT...

 It is safe to say that the title of this chapter really sums the subject up nicely. Taxes are, in fact, taxing! If you have a job, it is highly likely that you have to file taxes each year. If you are not filing taxes and are trying to "stick it to the man," I don't want to know! This is a book about how to successfully adult *legally*, no matter how tedious the task at hand may be. And in case you didn't get the memo, taxes are boring, in my humble, experienced opinion.

Grab yourself a caffeinated beverage and get ready to learn all about the magic of completing your taxes each and every year for the rest of your life. Before all of that fun, allow me to share with you a personal memory I have about filing taxes that I am actually quite fond of.

E. Z. DID IT!

My personal IRS relationship began when I got my first job and became responsible for filing my own taxes at the age of 15. I am about to sound super-old right now, but back in my day, taxes were completed by hand and filed through the mail, which is much more complicated than filing taxes these days with all the available online program options.

This process would have been even more challenging, had I not been lucky enough to have a tax-savvy momma to teach me what I needed to do. I have fond memories of sitting at the kitchen table with my mom and my tax documents. She had me fill everything out myself while offering help and guidance as needed to get the job done right, making sure I actually learned the process.

Fond memories involving filing taxes sounds weird — I am aware of that — but it was quality time spent with my mom, and I learned things about taxes that I have utilized every tax season since those early years. As you grow older, you become increasingly grateful for the time you spent with those you love most in this world, even if those times involved math.

I will not lie to you; filing taxes can be weird, confusing, and downright over-whelming sometimes. There are so many steps to follow and so much fine print to read, making it all too easy to mess up the math and forcing you to start all over. While I am aware not every young person is lucky enough to have a parent or guardian take on the role of their personal tax teacher, the bright side is that there are many online tax preparation programs out there that make filing a breeze. And, of course, I am here to help you too!

Programs break everything down in clear, easily understood steps, and if you still get confused during the process, a tax profes-sional is only a few clicks away to help you. I've been filing my taxes online for over 10 years now, and I can't say I miss the IRS booklets and their tiny print from the olden days!

WHAT'S IN IT FOR YOU!

While young people just learning about taxes have things much easier these days, it is still essential to understand the filing process and your options so you get the maximum return you deserve and you know how to properly protect your earnings from the ever-increasing population of scammers out there.

Use the information in this chapter to learn all about taxes and which methods you feel suit your wants and needs best. Keep in mind that if you try out one method or tax preparation program and are not fully satisfied with it, then try a new route the next time. Continue this until you find the perfect match for you.

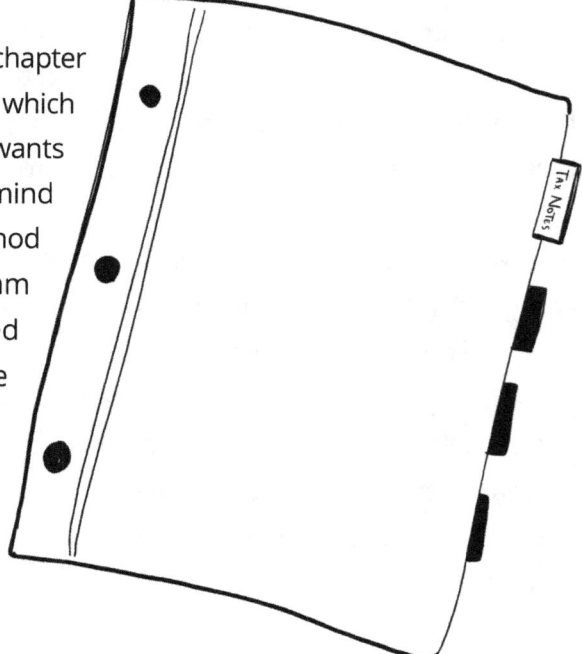

TYPES OF TAX FORMS

YAY, more forms! There's a different tax form
for every stage of life... yippy!

You will need different **forms and personal information** to properly file your taxes each year. The combination of these will vary depending on your life stage and the responsibilities you have taken on. Here is a quick form breakdown:

1040EZ: Basic tax form used by individuals or married couples with no dependents (children). Taxable income must be below $50,000.

1040A: Similar to the 1040EZ but allows you to claim more credits (education credits, child tax credit, etc.). Taxable income must be below $50,000.

Forms and Personal Information: Here is a list of common things you will need to file your taxes properly:

- Social security number
- Income source forms or unemployment form
- Mortgage statement
- Copy of last year's tax returns
- Financial account information

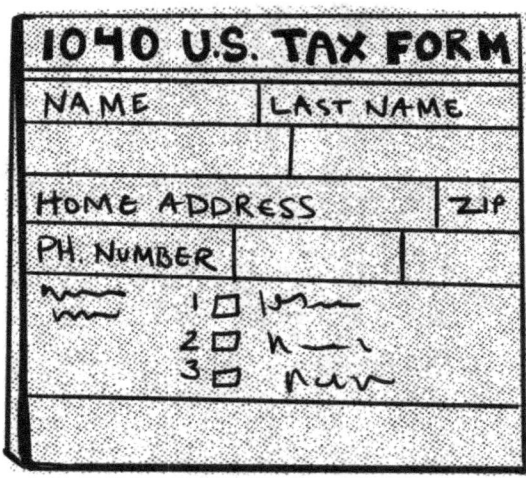

1040: This form is used if you make a taxable income over $50,000, need to itemize deductions, are reporting self-employment income, or reporting income from a property sale.

W-2: Wage and tax statement form that your employer supplies.
- Remember, your employer must send this out to you no later than January 31. *It is the law!*
- If your employer gives you the option to receive your W-2 by mail or electronically, you will typically receive it quicker if you pick the electronic delivery option.

W-4 (aka Employee's Withholding Certificate): The W-4 tells your employer how much tax to withhold from your check and needs to be filled out anytime you start a new job.

1099-NEC (Nonemployee Compensation): This form is used to calculate tax liability for self-employed people.

1098-T: This is a tuition statement going over the education expenses for the years you are a student. The information on this form determines if you will receive any education tax credit refunds and how much.

1098: Homeowners, business owners, or **sole proprietors** who are still paying on their mortgages and received at least $600 in mortgage interest during the year will need to file form 1098.

A EMPLOYEE'S SOCIAL SECURITY NUMBER		IRS E-FILE	
B EMPLOYER ID. NUMBER		1. WAGES, TIPS; E+C	2. FEDERAL INCOME TAX WITHHELD
C EMPLOYER'S NAME, ADDRESS, AND ZIPCODE		3. SOCIAL SECURITY WAGES	4. SOCIAL SECURITY WITHHELD
		5. MEDICARE WAGES + TIPS	6. MEDICARED TAX WITHHELD
		7. SOCIAL SECURITY TIPS	8 ALLOCATED TIPS
D CONTROL NUMBER		9.	10. DEPENDENT CARE BENEFITS
E EMPLOYEE'S FIRST NAME + INITIAL LAST NAME Suffix		11. NONQUALIFIED PLANS	12A. SEE BOX 12
		13. EMPLOYEE RETIREMENT PLAN 3RD PARTY SICK-PAY	12B.
		14. OTHER	12C.
			12D.
F EMPLOYEE'S ADDRESS + ZIPCODE			
15 STATE EMPLOYER'S STATE ID NUMBER	16 STATE WAGES; TIPS	17 STATE INCOME TAX	18 LOCAL WAGES; TIPS	19 LOCAL INCOME TAX	LOCALITY NAME

FORM **W-2** WAGE AND TAX STATEMENT   2022

Sole Proprietor: This term refers to an individual who owns an unincorporated business, runs it by themself, and pays personal income tax on business profits.

WAYS TO FILE

Whichever way you choose, you best file before Tax Day!

There are three main ways you can file your taxes each year: completing and mailing forms that you fill out by hand, using an online tax preparation program, or hiring a tax professional. The following is a quick breakdown of these three options:

- **Completing forms by hand** and mailing them to the IRS is an outdated option and should only really be used as a last resort, as this process takes much longer. The IRS encourages people to file electronically if possible.
- There are a variety of **online tax filing programs** you can use. For legality purposes, I will not name names, but some of the top options will play their commercials nonstop during tax season. You can't miss them!
  - ◊ Research your options to ensure you are using the best service for your needs or budget.
  - ◊ Check out the programs that offer free filing of basic tax forms or discounts to ensure you get the best deal.
- **Hiring a professional tax preparer** is a good idea if you have a more challenging tax return for some reason or feel completely overwhelmed and confused by the process, and there is no shame in feeling that way.
  - ◊ This can be a costly option, but keep in mind that most online tax programs offer assistance from a professional, if need be; there will likely be a small upcharge.

No matter which filing option you choose, DOUBLE-CHECK all information CAREFULLY before submitting your taxes. You could end up missing something and losing out on a chunk of money you should've gotten back, or you could miss something and end up not paying the proper amount of taxes you may owe. TAKE YOUR TIME; DO IT RIGHT!

TAX OVERVIEW & TIPS

Tackle those feelings of taxation evasion! You got this!

Taxes are something you cannot avoid and must do every year, which I know I have already said, but it is important enough to repeat, if you ask me. Here are a few more fun-filled taxing tips you will want to keep in mind each year:

- You can do your taxes once you receive your W-2s or 1099s and any other financial documents needed to file correctly.
- By law, your place of employment must provide you with your W-2 by the end of January, and taxes must be done by April 15 every year.

  - ◊ Please note: Tax due dates can change. The deadline was extended in 2021 and 2022 due to the pandemic madness. Pay attention!
  - ◊ Also, the deadline can shift if it falls on a holiday or weekend.
- Taxes get a bit trickier as you become a more *established adult* (i.e., homeowner, multiple financial accounts, donations, student loans, etc.). You will need to use different financial documents to complete your taxes depending on your different life factors at that time.
- Here's something important to know and remember: If you work or reside within the limits of a city that charges municipal taxes, you will likely have to pay extra taxes.
  - ◊ This is the case in St. Louis. I've had many loved ones learn this lesson the hard way when they ended up owing a bunch

of money in extra taxes — money they had already spent in many cases!

    ◊ If you or your employer forget to properly address this tax and make sure the taxes come out of your paychecks, it's a rude awakening a couple of years later when the IRS catches the mistake. One way or the other, you will pay!

    ◊ When getting a new job in a new state, county, city, etc., ask your employer about any extra taxes you would be responsible for paying if you accepted a position to work with them.

        + This would be a GREAT question to ask during an interview!

- Make sure you do not submit your taxes until you have received all the forms needed.

    ◊ Keeping a checklist of all the paperwork and forms you need is always a good idea to help you stay on top of things.

- If you are a student paying for your own college tuition, research the up-to-date tuition tax breaks that you may be eligible to receive on your yearly return.

    ◊ Tax breaks such as the American Opportunity Tax Credit and Lifetime Learning Credit can increase your tax return by a couple thousand dollars if you qualify.

- Different establishments will send out statements or forms you need for your taxes that state interest paid and other important monetary values that may be claimed on your taxes.

    ◊ Examples include bank statements listing earned interest through the year, personal property tax receipts, Form 1098 if you are paying interest on a mortgage, donation receipts, financial account statements, etc.

FRAUD ALERT!

The earlier you can file your taxes, the better, as these days, many people
will try to steal your tax returns.
REMEMBER — THE IRS WILL NEVER CALL YOU!
IRS CALLS ARE A SCAM! A SCAM, I SAY!

TAXES ARE TAXING
POP QUIZ!

Who doesn't love a pop quiz? Especially one where there are no wrong answers?!

There is not much to question and ponder in this chapter. To sum it all up, taxes are, in fact, taxing. Take the time to learn how to properly file for your present life situation, and make sure you are getting every drop of hard-earned money back that you earned and deserve.

Use the space below to jot down whatever notes you need to help you keep track of your tax filing obligations.

This would be a great place to make that list of tax forms and documents you will need!

Use this space to start planning out your journey to adulting happiness!

_____

_____

_____

_____

_____

_____

_____

_____

_____

_____

_____

_____

_____

_____

_____

_____

You Don't *Need* to Be Perfect, Just Insured

I ruin vacations.

NOBODY CAN PROTECT YOU AS WELL AS YOU CAN...
BESIDES THE RIGHT INSURANCE PLANS, THAT IS!

Insurance is important. You will hear this repeated several times throughout this chapter. All of the significant responsibilities one gets to experience in their adulting journey typically have some type of insurance and liability connected with them — everything from owning or renting a dwelling or vehicle to ensuring you stay happy and healthy.

It is crucial to remember that all insurance companies and types are not created equally or equitably. Doing your research and making educated decisions regarding your options on this matter can save you from having to navigate a whole lot of stress later on when it comes time to use your insurance.

E. Z. DID IT!

I have utilized all the necessary insurances a person needs to avoid complete financial ruin too many times to count at this point in my life. I have made many insurance-related decisions that have worked out in my favor and some that did not. Regardless of the outcome, every time I hear the word "deductible" or read the insanely high costs of medical care that have been billed to my insurance, my eye involuntarily twitches.

Be prepared to most likely become completely frustrated and annoyed with the way health care works in our country. That is a rant for a whole different book idea I have, though, and I will leave it at that. Just keep in mind, the more you learn about the insurance game, the less likely you will be to get played by it.

WHAT'S IN IT FOR YOU!

Insurance is essential, and understanding the proper insurance options you need to protect yourself and maintain your desired lifestyle is vital. Knowing the exact type of coverage you carry can keep you from making expensive errors. Insurance agents don't typically sympathize with those who mistakenly misunderstand their coverage; they just want their money.

I recommend you pay close attention to this chapter, so *their* money does not consist of all *your* money!

INSURANCE IS IMPORTANT
Keep in mind that insurance equals assurance!

Once you are moved out and on your own, you will be responsible for obtaining and paying for your insurance policies. There are several types of insurance you need to know about to keep yourself protected, including:

- Medical insurance
- Auto insurance
- Homeowners or renters insurance
- Life insurance (You shouldn't have to worry about it for a while, but it's something to think about.)
- Insurance to protect the money you've spent on things such as travel and material possessions

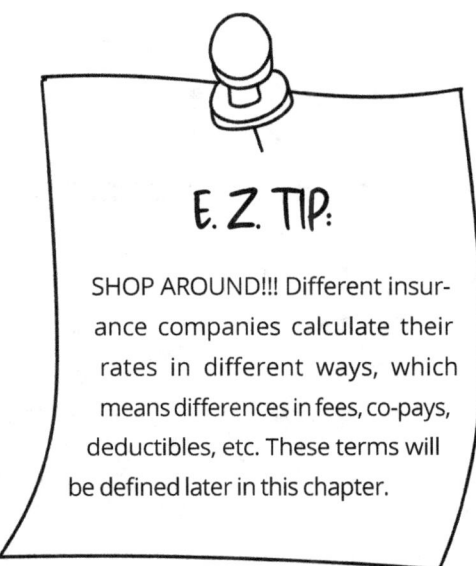

E. Z. TIP:

SHOP AROUND!!! Different insurance companies calculate their rates in different ways, which means differences in fees, co-pays, deductibles, etc. These terms will be defined later in this chapter.

Shopping around and comparing rates can save you A LOT of money!

I have my mom to thank for this tip. She may have annoyed me at times by ranting about the benefits of figuring out ALL of your options. Still, I am big enough to admit that when I have actually put in the work to gather new **quotes** from competing companies, I have always ended up saving money or finding a better policy for a similar price. My mom is the queen of saving money, and I was trained by the best. Thanks, Ma!

Quotes: An insurance quote is an estimate of the premium you would have to pay through that company. Remember that the quote will fluctuate depending on the coverage options you choose. A quote is not a bill or a contract; you are free to get quotes from as many companies as you want until you find the right package for you.

CAR INSURANCE

Combine auto insurance with airbags to keep your body AND wallet as safe as possible!

Guess what? CAR INSURANCE IS IMPORTANT! Different types of car insurance cost different amounts and cover different issues. Make sure you pay *very* close attention to all the little policy option details. I can't stress that enough. The following is a breakdown of different insurance policy options:

- **Comprehensive:** This insurance covers the damage done to your vehicle and its contents, not just from traffic accidents but from many natural sources such as floods, tornadoes, and hurricanes.
    - ◊ For example, comprehensive coverage kicks in if your car is damaged in a storm.
    - ◊ This coverage is typically more expensive, but it better protects you.
- **Collision:** This insurance covers the damage to your vehicle when an accident is your fault.
    - ◊ Most lenders will require you to have both comprehensive and collision conversion for the duration of your loan.
- **Liability:** This insurance covers any damage to other vehicles you're legally obligated to cover.
    - ◊ This coverage is cheaper, but you will pay a TON out of pocket if your car is damaged.
- **Uninsured & underinsured:** These are two policy options to consider if you can afford them to protect yourself further.
    - ◊ **Uninsured motorist coverage:** This type of coverage will protect the policyholder, the person whose name is on the card,

if they are in an accident with somebody who does not have insurance.

> + This is typically an option you can add to your standard policy coverage. It can cover both injuries and damage to your vehicle, and it can also cover you if you are on the receiving end of a hit-and-run accident.

◊ **Underinsured motorist coverage:** This type of coverage is needed for those who get into an accident with a driver whose **liability insurance limits** are too low to cover medical costs for people who have suffered injuries. For this insurance to kick in, you, the policyholder, cannot be the at-fault party responsible for causing the accident.

Remember: The higher the deductible, the lower the policy cost, but if you get into an accident, you will owe more money **out-of-pocket** to meet the deductible. Be sure to figure your insurance deductibles into your budget.

Liability Insurance Limits: Liability-only insurance pays for any damage and injuries the policyholder is responsible for. The limit of the policy is the highest amount of money the insurance company will cover; if costs go over that limit, the policyholder will be responsible for paying off the remainder.

Please note that insurance limits and coverage requirements can differ depending on what state you register your car in.

For example, these are the minimum liability coverage requirements for Missouri drivers:
- $25,000 per person for any bodily injuries
- $25,000 per accident for property damage
- $50,000 per accident for any bodily injuries

To find your state's insurance requirements, go to that state's Department of Revenue site.

Out-of-Pocket: Out-of-pocket costs are charges that you will be responsible for paying. Typically, an out-of-pocket cost needs to be paid in order for services to be done. You may be able to make payments, depending on the situation. Out-of-pocket costs are a great reason to make sure you put money into an emergency fund whenever possible.

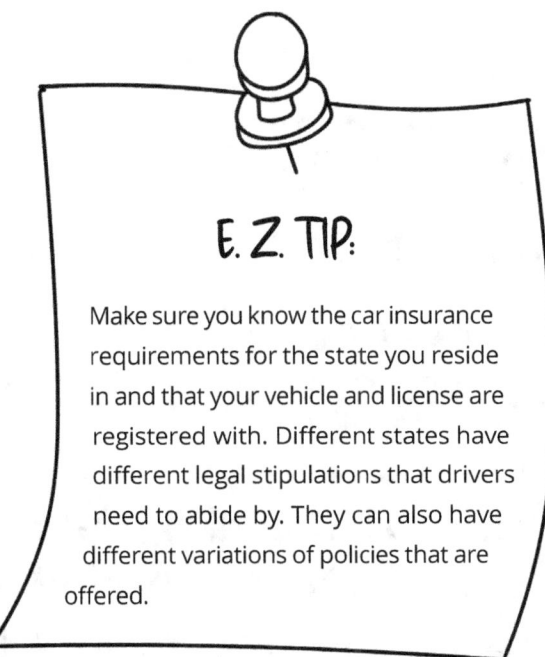

E. Z. TIP:

Make sure you know the car insurance requirements for the state you reside in and that your vehicle and license are registered with. Different states have different legal stipulations that drivers need to abide by. They can also have different variations of policies that are offered.

If you are caught not complying with your state's car insurance requirements, be prepared to deal with the consequences. If you have been paying attention, you are likely aware that consequences in the world of adulting tend to have price tags attached to them!

STEPS TO FINDING YOUR STATE'S MOTOR VEHICLE INSURANCE REQUIREMENTS:

① OPEN YOUR FAVORITE SEARCH ENGINE & TYPE "(YOUR STATE)'S CAR INSURANCE REQUIREMENTS" AND HIT THE SEARCH BUTTON.

② YOU WANT TO LOOK FOR YOUR STATE'S GOVERNMENT SITE TO GET THE CORRECT INFORMATION. CLICK ON THE SITE LINK ENDING IN ".GOV."

③ THIS SHOULD BRING YOU TO THE SITE SECTION THAT YOU NEED; MAKE SURE YOU READ AND UNDERSTAND EACH AND EVERY REQUIREMENT.

➡ IF IT DOESN'T PULL UP THE PAGE YOU NEED, TYPE "MOTOR VEHICLE INSURANCE" ON THE SITE'S SEARCH BAR, WHICH SHOULD PULL UP THE INFORMATION YOU NEED.

MEDICAL INSURANCE

Health insurance gives you some immunity against those big medical bills!

Most full-time jobs offer medical insurance as part of their **benefits package** and will automatically deduct the costs from your wages. Different medical needs typically require different types of insurance or coverage (i.e., dental, vision, basic medical).

Not all employers offer all types of medical insurance, so make sure you know what is being covered by your employer policy and if you need to get further insured by other means.

Without insurance, medical fees are EXTREMELY COSTLY. Medical insurance coverage is VERY IMPORTANT. Are you picking up on my oh-so-subtle hints on the importance of insurance yet?

Benefits Package: The exact components and costs of an employee package plan can greatly differ depending on factors such as the company you work for and extra people added to your coverage.

The average full-benefits package for a person employed through a company full-time includes health, dental, and vision coverage as well as short-term and long-term disability insurance, worker's compensation, life insurance, Social Security, Medicare, retirement plans, and paid time off (PTO).

If your job doesn't offer insurance, you will need to get yourself insured on your own ASAP. Many companies offer health insurance plans for you to purchase if your employer doesn't offer one. Take the time to research current healthcare policies and plans available at the present time to find the option that best suits what you need.

- healthcare.gov is a great site to find the most current options in healthcare insurance and needs.

INSURANCE VOCAB:

Co-pays: It is important to remember that you will likely still have out-of-pocket expenses even when you are fully insured. Typically, you will have to pay a co-pay fee upfront for each medical appointment you go to.

- The fee varies depending on what type of appointment it is (i.e., general practitioner, specialist, ER, etc.) and who your insurer is.
- The average medical co-pay cost falls between $15 and $50.

Deductible: A specified amount of money you must pay before your insurance company pays a claim, which varies by insurer. Most insurance companies will send you a bill after your medical provider sends them an account of services rendered.

- It is your responsibility to pay the deductible amount for that year, then your insurance will cover costs for the remainder of the year.
- Keep in mind that you will still be responsible for appointment co-pays even after you've met your deductible.

- The average deductible for a single person falls in the $1,000-to-$1,500 range and goes up significantly for family coverage.

Premium: This is the amount you pay each month for your insurance coverage.

- Keep in mind that healthcare plan benefits for a new job typically do not kick in until you've been employed for a certain period of time (i.e., six months).

REMEMBER! Health insurance requirements can vary depending on the type of coverage you have, how many people you need to be covered, and what state you live in. Co-pay, deductible, and premium amounts can be vastly different as well.

Under current law, you can stay on your parent's insurance until you are 26 years old, then you are responsible for obtaining your own. Please note this law can change depending on the political climate at the time.

Also, keep in mind that insurance policy requirements and options can vary by state, so make sure you do your medical insurance research for the state you reside in.

MEDICAL INSURANCE PLAN TYPES:

Health Maintenance Organizations (HMO): This plan provides all health services through a network of specified providers and facilities. HMO holders have little freedom to choose providers and are required to see a primary doctor before being referred to any type of specialist.

- If you see a provider that is not in your HMO network, you will likely be responsible for the entire bill.

Preferred Provider Organizations (PPO): This plan offers more freedom over health care than an HMO, and you can see a specialist without needing a referral.

- You will pay more money upfront for an out-of-network provider, though.

Exclusive Provider Organization (EPO): This plan also offers more freedom of healthcare choices than an HMO. You also can see a specialist without a referral.

- This plan's premium is less than a PPO; however, they cover zero costs for out-of-network providers.

Point-of-Service (POS) plan: This type of plan is a hybrid of an HMO and a PPO in that you have a good level of freedom when choosing a healthcare option, and you will have a primary doctor who coordinates your care and refers you to specialists.

- You will also pay more to see a care provider not in your network.

Dental & vision: The coverage for these needs will differ depending on your insurance. Most plans with these coverage options provide two dental cleanings a year with an allotted amount of dental work and one yearly eye exam.

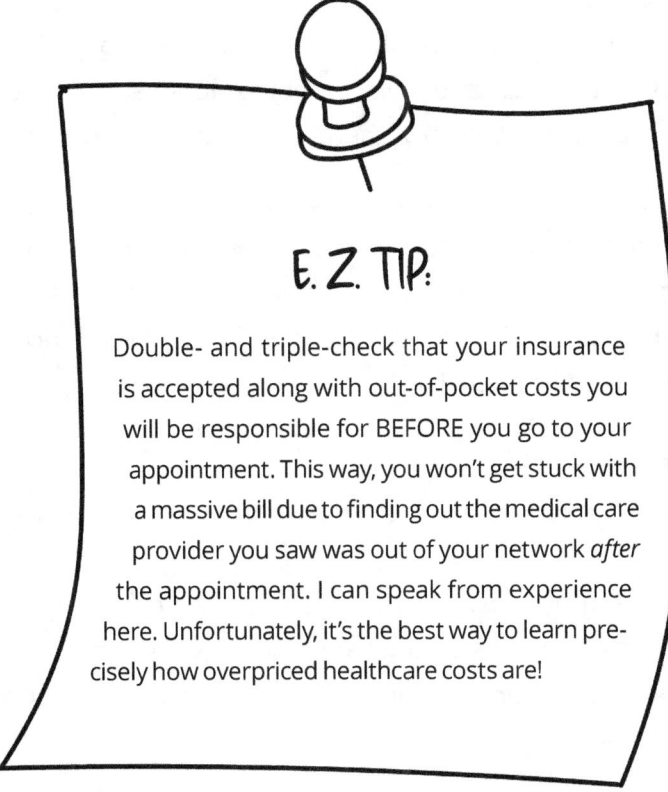

E. Z. TIP:

Double- and triple-check that your insurance is accepted along with out-of-pocket costs you will be responsible for BEFORE you go to your appointment. This way, you won't get stuck with a massive bill due to finding out the medical care provider you saw was out of your network *after* the appointment. I can speak from experience here. Unfortunately, it's the best way to learn precisely how overpriced healthcare costs are!

HOMEOWNERS & RENTERS INSURANCE

You can never have too much security when it comes to protecting your home!

Homeowner and renter insurances are extremely critical to protect yourself and your belongings when life happens.

I bet you thought I would say it was important, didn't you? It *is* important, though, so pay close attention!

- This type of insurance, depending on the policy options you choose, will help cover costs to repair or replace your belongings or home in the event of perils such as theft, fire, or other natural disasters.

> **Side note:** When buying a home, do your research to make sure your property is not on a flood plain. Insurance companies typically do not offer flood insurance in areas known to flood.

- Make sure you know what is covered under your policy *before* needing it.
- Double-check that you have some type of coverage to protect yourself in the instance that somebody injures themselves on your property and decides to sue. We live in a sue-happy society these days!

- If you purchase costly new appliances or other items for your home, don't forget to increase your insurance premiums to reflect that and ensure you have the proper coverage.
- Again, SHOP AROUND! Rates can greatly differ depending on the property, coverage type, location, and cost of items you wish to insure.

TAKE THE TIME TO UNDERSTAND YOUR INSURANCE POLICY AND YOUR RIGHTS!
Try and learn from my experiences in hopes that you avoid finding yourself in a similar situation!

PREAMBLE TO THE PROBLEM

Fun fact: This story you are about to read was a (very) last-minute addition to the manuscript. It's a doozy of a story, and most definitely worth reading.

As you may be aware by now, insurance is a tricky beast, filled with clauses and policies that may not make sense and that may not rule in your favor. However, that is life: just because something does not sound right or fair, that does not mean you can ignore it and make up your own rules. Adulting does *not* work that way.

Homeowners insurance operates much differently from auto insurance in that the person who has "caused" the problem may not necessarily be the one having to file the insurance claim to cover damages that occurred to another person's property. I had known this rule only because a good friend of mine had to go through it when a tree on their property fell into their neighbor's yard during a storm, causing damage.

It was determined that the tree was healthy when it fell, and because of this, the neighbor whose property was damaged had to make the claim through their insurance. The incident was deemed "an act of God." Yes, that is a real insurance claim that refers to a natural event that was caused due to no fault of humans. Had the tree been dead when it fell, the tree owner would have to make the claim due to negligence for not maintaining their property. Weird, right?

Unfortunately, their neighbor refused to believe they were required to settle this matter through *their insurance*, and they had to deal with a lot of negative backlash from them. The situation I have been dealing with is on the same spectrum as that.

To read the rest of this whirlwind tale, head to the back of the book and look for the "Insurance Nightmare Bonus Story." Make sure you buckle up first; you're in for a weird and wild insurance story!

YOU DON'T *NEED* TO BE PERFECT, JUST INSURED POP QUIZ!

Who doesn't love a pop quiz? Especially one where there are no wrong answers?!

Read each question and really take the time to ponder the answers — not how you *THINK* you should answer, but how you *WANT* to answer! Use the blank space below to write down your answers or anything you'd like. It is your book, after all!

E. Z. TIP:

To make this book personal to your life, write down your answers in the area provided and leave yourself some space to revamp your responses as you experience the different twists and turns of your adulting journey.

QUIZ QUESTIONS

1. What state do you live in? What are the car insurance requirements for that state? This answer can be found by going to your state's Department of Revenue website.

2. What are the medical insurance requirements for your state? Go to HealthCare.gov to easily find this answer.

3. Think about both your personal health and family health history. Are there any potential medical conditions you may be more prone to getting? If yes, ensure your policy is customized to suit your needs before a potential issue may arise.

4. What valuables and property do you want to make sure you protect when finding the best homeowners or renters insurance policies? What is the estimated value of these items?

5.   Did you get quotes from multiple insurance companies to find the best policy and rate for you? Use the note space below to write down the company name, insurance quote amount, and policy details for each place you contacted; that way, you can update it as you go through life changes and ensure you are maintaining the best insurance options to suit your needs.

Use this space to start planning out your journey to adulting happiness!

_____

_____

_____

_____

_____

_____

_____

_____

_____

_____

_____

Obtaining & Maintaining a Sweet Ride!

PHONES DOWN AND EYES ON THE ROAD:
THE KEY TO ENSURING YOU ARRIVE ALIVE.

When it comes to cars, people have different feelings about them. Some see them as a simple mode of transportation; others see them as status symbols. I love cars for a multitude of reasons. An exciting part about being an adult is getting to make choices on what you deem important, and your transportation choices are most definitely something that you will need to put a lot of thought into.

This subject is full of fond, personal memories, and I am delighted to share some of my favorites with you. Pay close attention to this story to learn some important lessons that apply to all facets of life.

E. Z. DID IT!

As far back as I can remember, my dad had a love of cars. He always enjoyed test-driving different models and styles that piqued his curiosities and going to the big car show held in our city each year. I can't peg down an exact date or moment in my life when I began to share the love and appreciation of an exemplary vehicle just like my dad did, but soon enough, I began to join him on test-drive excursions and would take off work to be his car show buddy. Taking a day off work to make meaningful memories with loved ones is never a bad thing (in moderation). Please don't let people make you feel like it is.

Being surrounded by all those shiny rides of every shape, color, size, and model just made me happy, and it still does. Not to mention testing out the horsepower of a sports car on the highway or playing with a four-wheel-drive

SUV in a snow-covered parking lot is a blast! I saw a car as a way to express myself, telling people what I'm about before they even know me. Though what other people thought has never really been a priority for me, what mattered most was how that car made *me* feel. Live your life for yourself, not others.

My true love of cars manifested itself shortly after buying my very first whip (as the kids like to say), a Grand Prix. She was a beauty, and she was all mine; I was so proud to drive it and so proud of the fact I was working and paying it off myself. Slowly I started adding my own personal touches to my new car child: tinted windows, a leather "bra" wrap on the front hood, a custom monogram decal on the back windshield, and a brightly colored flower lei dangling from my rearview mirror.

When I close my eyes, I swear I can still feel the steering wheel in my hands and hear my obnoxiously loud music pumping through the speakers. It was a feeling of freedom I had never felt up to that point. Owning my car always left me with a strong sense of fulfillment — maybe because it was the first substantial "adult" thing I owned, or perhaps because of the many fond memories I have shared with my dad over our mutual love of cars.

I have been driving and owning cars for over 17 years, which makes me feel super-old, especially considering that 17 is the target audience age for this book! Seventeen years and seven cars later, I learned a lesson from each one. The Grand Prix taught me to take pride in working hard and paying for my own things. I traded in the Grand Prix for an Eclipse; that was the car love of my life.

At the time, I was working two jobs and going to college full-time. It was during one of the times I played hooky and took off to go to the car show with my dad when I first laid eyes on a shiny, orange Eclipse on the showroom floor. It was love at first sight. A few weeks later, I found a used orange Eclipse with all the bells and whistles, and she became mine.

Our love affair was intense and, unfortunately, short-lived, as I totaled her after I hydroplaned on the highway a little over a year after she came into my life. I mourned that vehicle like I had lost a best friend. I was so focused on my "baby" that it took me a long time to actually realize how very close I had been to dying and how lucky I was to have walked away unscathed from such a horrible accident.

To this day, I still have an insane level of anxiety when driving or riding in a car through the pouring rain. With that experience under my belt, my Eclipse taught me to take a step back and realize that a car is just a car. It can be replaced, and I cannot be. So, while I've enjoyed my vehicles since the Eclipse, I am overly aware that they are replaceable material objects and should be treated as such.

Maybe you have a similar love of cars or maybe you don't; how you choose to feel about the subject is totally okay. Regardless of your feelings, if you own a car, you should understand how to handle and care for it appropriately. Before you buy a new or new-to-you vehicle, DO YOUR RESEARCH!

One of my favorite ways to research a vehicle I am interested in is to look up consumer reviews; I want to hear real stories from real people rather than putting my trust in big-name reviewers who probably make their own snap judgments and then drive home in their Lambos.

Something else to always keep in mind is that *car* people tend to think their chosen car brand is the best type and the only one you should drive, hands down, no question. Does that make them right? It does for that person, but it does not have to be the correct answer for you. Never let somebody peer-pressure you into making a decision you are not entirely comfortable with, whether with a significant purchase like a new car or any other avenue of life.

Test-drive anything and everything, find out as many details regarding the vehicle's history as possible, ask questions, look over every inch of that car, and never put your full trust in a car salesperson. You do not want to come into a purchase as big as this without doing your own **vehicle research**. Ultimately, the sale is their job, not your satisfaction, and selling you that car is putting money in their pockets. Don't hate the player; hate the game!

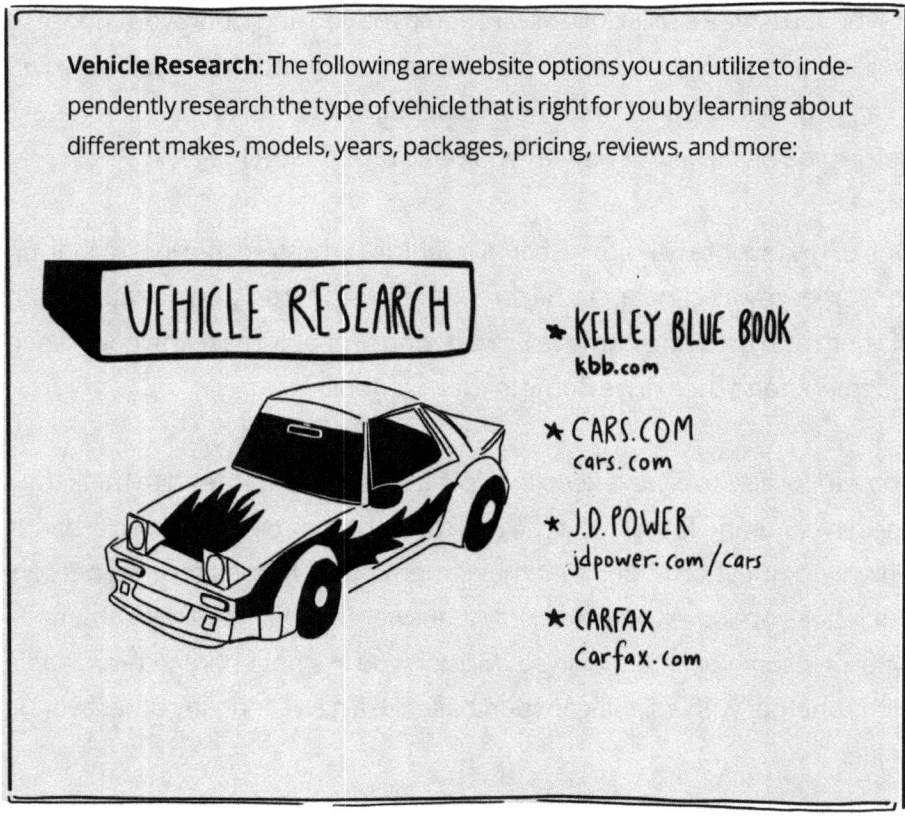

Vehicle Research: The following are website options you can utilize to independently research the type of vehicle that is right for you by learning about different makes, models, years, packages, pricing, reviews, and more:

VEHICLE RESEARCH

★ KELLEY BLUE BOOK
kbb.com

★ CARS.COM
cars.com

★ J.D. POWER
jdpower.com/cars

★ CARFAX
carfax.com

Typing these last few paragraphs brought back vivid memories of test-driving cars with my dad that we were actually considering purchasing. We would test-drive them home "to show Mom" and then proceed to check every nook and cranny of that vehicle's interior and exterior; I'm talking lying on the driveway, getting dirty, detailed inspections. If it passed the "Dad inspection," then we would take it back and start the negotiation process.

Knowing the actual value of that car and what you are willing to pay for it is a critical factor in the song and dance that is the car-buying process. Most times, negotiations were successful, and we left in a new ride, and other times, the dealer wouldn't budge on the price, and we walked away. Once I was haggling with a dealer on this Nitro SUV that I was in love with (pro tip: never let a dealer see that you are in love); the salesman wasn't giving me the number I wanted, so as much as I was disappointed, I got up and started to leave. The salesman proceeded to chase me down, handed me a bottle of water, and told me to sit tight while he went back and talked to the "boss."

It turned out he could get to the number I wanted; it was clear that he just didn't expect a young woman to be so educated about vehicles and the purchase process. That Nitro was the number one favorite of all the vehicles I have owned thus far, at least where proper human-material possession etiquette is concerned. Sometimes a car is just a car; other times, a car can teach you lessons that will stick with you for the rest of your life.

WHAT'S IN IT FOR YOU!

Perhaps this chapter will teach you some new lessons about cars and life in general. Don't let people push you around. Make sure you walk or drive away from a situation knowing that you made the best choice for yourself and are satisfied with the outcome. Work hard for the things you want and hold your head high when those goals are achieved.

When it comes to navigating the world of adulting, you will find that there are new lessons to be learned with every curve of the road. The information in this chapter is meant to help you learn about the different options you may have in regard to owning (or leasing) a vehicle as well as some snazzy upkeep tips!

BUYING OR LEASING A VEHICLE

Pick the option you find most pleasing!

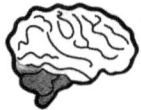

BUYING A VEHICLE: PROS & CONS

The pros:

- You are the owner of the vehicle; any **equity value** it retains can be used to purchase another vehicle when traded in.
- It is yours to drive how you please, customize, and handle repairs as you see fit.
- Financing is usually easier than leasing, though your credit score plays a major role here. You may also have the option to refinance your car loan, lower your payments, and save money.
- Once you have paid the vehicle off, you are done with monthly payments, and you own your car outright.

Equity Value: This is the monetary difference between the current value of the vehicle and the amount that is owed on the loan. If you have a positive equity value on your car, you can use that equity toward the purchase of another vehicle at trade-in. Making a large down payment on a vehicle, at least 20% of the cost, will help you stay ahead of depreciation and negative equity.

The cons:

- It is expensive up front, and payments are usually higher. You have to pay high sales taxes too.
- You are solely responsible for repairs and maintenance, which can be very expensive, depending on the type of vehicle and the warranty it comes with (or doesn't).
- Vehicle value can **depreciate** very quickly, and it is easy to be **upside down** on your car loan, meaning you owe more money than it is worth, making trade-in much more expensive.

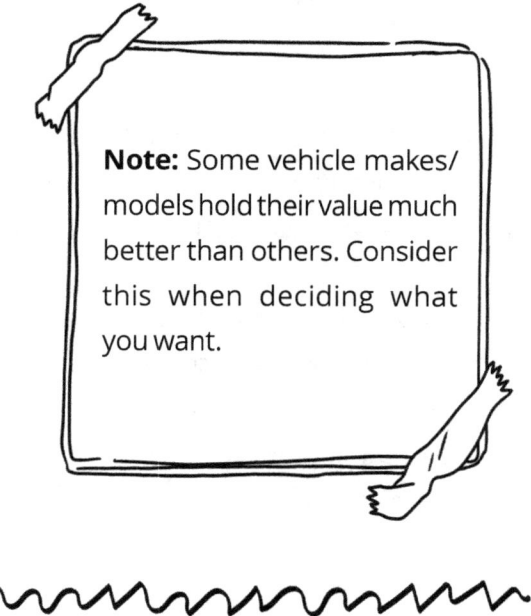

Note: Some vehicle makes/ models hold their value much better than others. Consider this when deciding what you want.

Depreciate: This is the decrease in value of an asset you own, such as a vehicle. The value of your car will decline in value the longer you own it and the more wear and tear that is put on it. On average, a vehicle's worth will decline by 20% in the first year you own it.

- Depreciation is an important factor to consider when deciding between buying a new or used car.

Upside Down: Being upside down on a loan means that you owe more on your property than it is worth; this would be considered negative equity. This is common in regard to auto loans, as the value is more likely to depreciate rapidly over a short amount of time.

- You can still trade in your vehicle for another one if you are upside down on the loan. Just keep in mind you are responsible for paying off the negative equity on your trade-in vehicle's loan.
  - ◊ Example: You owe $5,000 on your current car, and at trade-in, the dealer offers you $3,000, meaning you have a negative equity value of $2,000 that you are responsible for paying for.
- Many dealers will offer to roll your negative equity in with your new car loan. While this is convenient, you will likely be immediately upside down on your new car loan. This can put you back into financial hardship, so make sure you crunch all the numbers and update your budget to ensure you can handle the new payments.

LEASING A VEHICLE: PROS & CONS

The pros:
- You do not own the vehicle; you are technically just renting it for a specified amount of time, making trading it in easier.
- Payments tend to be lower, as you are paying for the estimated amount of depreciation likely to occur during your leasing term. You will likely save money on sales taxes as well.

- Leased vehicles are newer, meaning you will (hopefully) not have to deal with any repair issues and will get to drive a vehicle with newer technology.
    ◊ Many newer cars come with extra perks such as free oil changes and basic maintenance services; make sure you inquire about this before leasing.
- You will likely be driving a vehicle that is going to have some type of warranty coverage on it.

The cons:
- Some leasing companies may require you to pay a down payment first.
- If you do not abide by the lease agreement regarding the vehicle's condition and mileage, you can get slammed with penalty fees. While

you have to pay if you go over the mileage that was agreed upon, you do not get credit for any unused miles you may have at trade-in.

- As long as you are leasing a vehicle, you will be making monthly payments.
- If, for some reason, you are not happy with the vehicle you are leasing and bring it back to the dealer, you can get stuck with huge penalty fees.
- You will likely still be required to pay for maintenance such as new tires.
- READ THE FINE PRINT on the leasing contract to ensure you understand what is covered and what is not!

VEHICLE FEES & WARRANTIES

As if owning a ride wasn't expensive enough, don't forget to budget these extra fees!

When purchasing a new or new-to-you vehicle, consider the other fees you will be responsible for paying so you don't end up with a massive amount of debt you were not expecting. Also, make sure that you fully understand the warranty options that come with the vehicle or can be purchased with it, as this factor can save you money as well — or not, if you purchase bogus coverage.

The following are additional expenses that may come with buying a vehicle:

Note: Fees differ depending on the state you live in or purchase the vehicle in, what type of vehicle is purchased, whether you traded in your old vehicle to purchase the new one, etc.

- Registration processing/ transfer fees
- State sales tax
- Title fee
- Title processing fee
- Transfer fee

For more detailed information regarding buying a vehicle, locate the title and registration guidelines for the state you live in as well as the state you purchase the vehicle in if it is different from the state you reside in.

- For Missouri, go to this website: dor.mo.gov/forms/5687.pdf

- For other states, search "vehicle title and registration guidelines for (insert state here)."
  - ◊ Make sure you go to the site ending in .gov.

WARRANTY OVERVIEW:

A vehicle warranty is a contracted agreement from either the car's manufacturer or an aftermarket company that limits your financial risk for a specific period. It keeps you from having to pay too much money out-of-pocket; think of it as health insurance for your car. There are various types of warranties available, some better than others. The following is a breakdown of common warranty options and information.

- If you are buying a car brand new, there should be a warranty already rolled into the cost of the vehicle. Check your financial papers during the purchasing process to make sure the seller is not trying to sneak in an extra warranty fee.
- If you purchase a used car, it may still have the warranties it came with when it was purchased new, as most warranties stay with that vehicle even after ownership transfers.
- **Warranty breakdown:** You will most commonly see warranties in this format: #X years/#X miles. This means that the warranty will last up to that

specific number of years or miles, whichever comes first. If you have a 5-year/50,000-mile warranty and you drive 50,001 miles in 4 years, your warranty period will have ended.

- A car warranty is NOT the same as car insurance; a warranty will not cover damage caused by an accident, weather, theft, and other outside factors that don't pertain directly to the quality of the vehicle. Warranties also typically do not cover any kind of routine maintenance the vehicle needs, such as oil changes.

- Most warranties will only cover damages that occurred from normal wear and tear or if the vehicle had defective parts. What exactly is covered will depend on the type of warranty the car has. The following are common options:

  ◊ **Powertrain warranty:** This should cover all of the mechanical parts that keep that vehicle moving. These warranties tend to last for several years; common powertrain coverage options are 5 years/60,000 miles up to 10 years/100,000 miles.

  ◊ **Comprehensive warranty:** Also called a bumper-to-bumper warranty, it should cover every part your vehicle had when it was purchased. This warranty has a shorter set time, typically around 3 years/36,000 miles.

  ◊ **Restraint systems warranty:** This covers any damage that occurs with your vehicle's safety features, its airbags, and seat belts. The time stipulations on this warranty type will greatly differ depending on the brand of vehicle you purchase; some manufacturers offer a seat belt warranty that covers the entire life of the car.

◊ **Extended warranty:** This option allows you to extend your vehicle's warranty once the warranties you bought it with have expired. These are typically offered through aftermarket companies, and the cost can greatly differ depending on the option you go with.

+ Make sure to THOROUGHLY research your extended warranty before purchasing it; this type of warranty tends to have a lot of scammers looking to sell you a useless warranty.

READ THE FINE PRINT BEFORE YOU SIGN!

BASIC VEHICLE UPKEEP

If your car doesn't run, then you are going to have to!

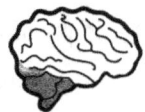

HOW TO CHANGE A TIRE

While I am a big fan of getting a AAA membership, knowing how to change a tire on your own *before* experiencing a blowout on the open road is essential. I highly recommend you practice this procedure in a safe spot with someone who is experienced to watch over you and provide guidance. Run through this procedure a few times to be sure you are comfortable doing it by yourself.

This can be dangerous if not done properly!

1. If you are driving and your tire blows, slowly reduce your speed, turn on your hazard lights, and look for a safe, level spot to pull over as far away from traffic as possible.
2. Get out the jack, tire wrench, and spare tire you should always keep in your car.
    ◊ Know where these items are BEFORE you need them!

3. If your car has hubcaps, you will need to carefully pry the cap off using the tire wrench or a large flat-blade screwdriver. Use the tire wrench to loosen the lug nuts on the flat tire to the point that you can turn them by hand.
    ◊ Remember: Lefty Loosey and Righty Tighty!
4. Place the jack under the car's frame, close to the flat tire. Make sure it is a metal frame part and not plastic. It is best to consult your car's manual for exact placement directions, as it should ALWAYS be in your car somewhere.
5. Use the jack to lift the car until the tire is off the ground, then remove the lug nuts and set them in a SAFE place.
6. Grab the tire on each side and remove it from the lug bolts by pulling it straight off, set it to the side, and mount the spare tire in its place.
7. Reinstall the lug nuts and screw them down hand-tight until seated against the wheel. Tighten the nuts in a star pattern — move to the

next nut across rather than one adjacent — to ensure the wheel mounts evenly. Use the tire wrench for one turn if you need to be sure the tire is secure but DO NOT completely tighten all the bolts while the tire is in the air.

8. Using the jack, lower the car until the tire is just touching the ground. Do not put the full weight of the car on the spare yet. Following the same star pattern as before, tighten the lug nuts with your tire wrench as much as possible.

9. If applicable, reinstall the hubcap. Lower the jack completely and remove it from the car frame.

> **Note:** Most spare tires in cars today are not full-size tires and should not be driven for long distances or at high speeds. Consult your car's manual for specific limits regarding your spare tire.

10. Using a tire gauge, check the tire pressure. If needed, add air with a portable tire inflator. If you do not have one, carefully drive to the nearest gas station.

11. Pack up your flat tire and bring it to a shop to see if it can be repaired, as that is usually cheaper than having to replace it.

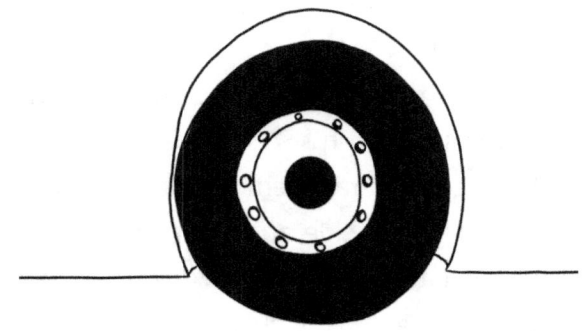

TIRE MAINTENANCE

Some vehicles may have built-in tire pressure sensors that will let you know when attention is needed, and some don't, making this a good skill to know and be prepared for. If you are driving on a flat, straight road, carefully take your hands off the steering wheel. If your car noticeably pulls in one direction, that likely means your tires are not evenly filled. If they are evenly filled and the car still pulls, there is likely a bigger issue going on, and you should take your car into the shop as soon as you can.

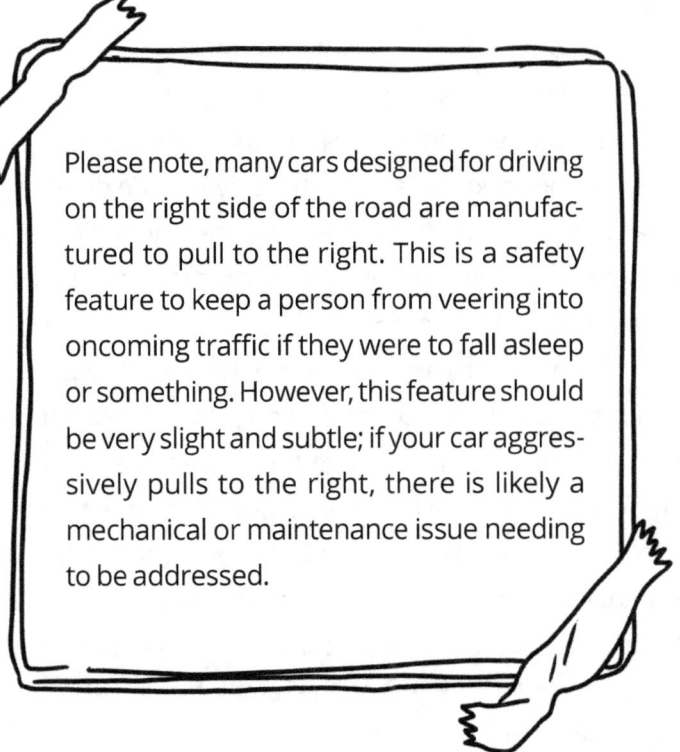

Please note, many cars designed for driving on the right side of the road are manufactured to pull to the right. This is a safety feature to keep a person from veering into oncoming traffic if they were to fall asleep or something. However, this feature should be very slight and subtle; if your car aggressively pulls to the right, there is likely a mechanical or maintenance issue needing to be addressed.

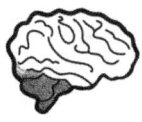

HOW TO CHECK TIRE PRESSURE

Keep in mind that the outside temperature can cause your tires' pressure to fluctuate. The colder it is, the denser the air is, and the more likely it will be that your tires will lose pressure. Warmer temperatures can raise the tire pressure, so if it's hot out, keep this in mind so you don't overinflate the tire. You will get the most accurate reading on your tire pressure BEFORE your car has been driven.

Purchase a reliable tire pressure gauge to keep in your car, and remember that you can find the recommended pounds per square inch (PSI) for your vehicle's tires on the sticker located on the driver's side doorframe or in the car's manual. Follow the procedure below to check your tire pressure:

1. Remove the valve cap from the valve stem on the tire you want to check and put it somewhere safe.
2. Place the pressure gauge over the valve stem and press down hard enough so the hissing sound disappears and your gauge provides a reading. With a standard gauge, the air pressure will push a small bar out from the bottom of the gauge. Measurement units are etched into the bar. A digital gauge will show you the reading on a screen. Repeat this step a few times to ensure you get an accurate reading.
3. Notate the pressure level that shows on the gauge.
4. Repeat steps 1 through 3 on the remaining tires. This would also be an excellent time to check the spare tire.

Check your tire pressure regularly, especially when there's a significant temperature change.

Adding air to tires: If you do not have access to an air compressor, they can be found at most gas stations. Keep in mind that compressors can operate differently and that you should FULLY read the directions for that specific one before using it. Use the compressor to add air to your tires, making sure you are pausing to check the PSI with your pressure gauge to avoid overinflation.

If you overinflate the tire, it is okay, as you can easily let the air out. Having a PSI that is too high can cause issues with things like road traction and tire wear-out.

If your gauge's PSI reading has dropped 10% or more, you need to add air. For example, if your car recommends a tire PSI of 40, any reading of 36 or below means you need to add air.

Removing air from tires: If need be, remove the valve cap from the tire and put it somewhere safe, then identify the metal pin located in the center of the valve.

Use a slender object like a screwdriver to push down on the metal pin. You will hear the air hissing loudly as it deflates the tire. Pause often to check the tire's PSI with your gauge and stop when the proper PSI is achieved.

CHECKING A VEHICLE'S FLUID LEVELS

Proper fluid intake is not only important to keep your body functioning properly, but your car as well. The following fluids play a vital role in maintaining a healthy, happy vehicle:

- **Oil:** This is one of the most vital fluids your car needs to run smoothly. With the help of your manual, pop the car's hood and locate the engine oil dipstick.
  - ◊ Please note: you will get a more accurate reading if you are able to test the oil either before the vehicle is driven or a minimum of 15 minutes after the engine had been shut off.
  - ◊ Remove the dipstick completely and wipe clean with a paper towel or something you don't mind being oil-stained.
  - ◊ Once totally clean, insert the dipstick fully back into place and then pull it back out. The oil measurement can be found on the tip of the dipstick. There will be a scale showing the maximum and minimum oil levels. You want the oil level to be close to the max level.
  - ◊ If the oil reading is low, make sure you add oil immediately and figure out if the car is leaking oil or just burning it off quickly. Different vehicle models will burn oil at different rates, so you need to learn how your specific car functions in order to best monitor it.
  - ◊ Rewipe the dipstick with a fresh, white paper towel and examine the oil quality. If the oil appears gritty or darker in color, it is time to change it.
  - ◊ Normal color oil should appear to be orange to yellow on the clean cloth.

- **Transmission fluid:** This fluid is about as important as the engine oil. It both lubricates and cools the car's transmission.
    - ◊ The first step is to read your car's manual and learn exactly what is needed to check this fluid; some can be checked with a dipstick similar to checking oil, some may not be able to be checked without a mechanic, and others can have a built-in sensor allowing you to easily check fluid levels.
    - ◊ If the transmission fluid level reading is low or appears dirty and gritty, you need to have the fluid added or flushed out and changed.
    - ◊ Normal transmission fluid should be a fairly dark red to orange, depending on type/brand.

- **Brake fluid:** If you are driving a car, you should already know that the brakes are essential. Brake fluid allows your car's braking system to function properly. If your brake pedal feels spongy instead of firm when applying the brakes, check the fluid level ASAP.
    - ◊ Again, consult your car's manual to learn how to check the brake fluid level for your vehicle.
    - ◊ If you check the fluid and it is low, add more as soon as possible. This fluid can vary in color, but it should always be transparent; dark/cloudy fluid should be replaced.

- **Windshield wiper fluid:** This fluid doesn't affect the car's operation, but it does affect yours! You need to see to drive.
  - ◊ Consult your car's manual to learn where the wiper fluid reservoir is located.
  - ◊ If the fluid level is low, add more; wiper fluid is cheap and easy to find.

- **Coolant fluid (aka antifreeze):** Just like you are staying cool, your vehicle needs to as well. This fluid will help keep your engine from overheating.
  - ◊ Your car's manual will tell you how to check your engine's coolant accurately.
  - ◊ For the most accurate reading, make sure your car is parked on level ground and the engine compartment is completely cooled down.
  - ◊ Open your hood and locate your radiator and coolant reservoir. The reservoir should be clear plastic, so you can easily see the level of coolant and the maximum fill line.

◊ If the fluid level is low or the color looks dirty, you must add or replace fluid as directed. If your coolant is colorless, rust-colored, has particles, or is oily or sludgy, you'll want to have it inspected by your local mechanic. These are all signs of contamination that may indicate more severe issues.

- **Power steering fluid:** Power steering is a luxury that is very underappreciated, and your car needs to have this fluid in order to maintain this crucial function.

    ◊ Though I am sure you can guess what I am going to say, I will repeat myself once more: READ YOUR CAR'S MANUAL! This will teach you how to locate this fluid reservoir in the engine compartment. Carefully read the directions and then check the level.

    ◊ If levels are low, top them off; if dirty, flush and replace.

E. Z. FLUID TIPS:

Make sure you know the exact brands and types of fluids needed by your specific vehicle; check and double-check this information BEFORE pouring any fluids anywhere. Keep a slip of paper with all this information in your glove box so it is handy when you need it.

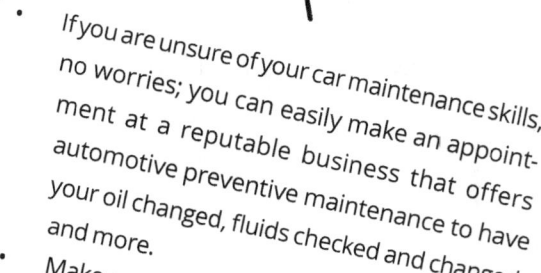

- If you are unsure of your car maintenance skills, no worries; you can easily make an appointment at a reputable business that offers automotive preventive maintenance to have your oil changed, fluids checked and changed, and more.
- Make sure to add vehicle maintenance fees into your budget and find an online coupon before you go.
- There is ALWAYS a coupon. If you can't find a coupon for the specific place you want to go to, most places will accept coupons from competitors as well.

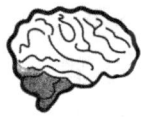

STEPS FOR CHANGING YOUR CAR'S OIL

Just like you should be doing for any project, the first step is to gather all the necessary supplies BEFORE you begin. Necessary oil change supplies include the correct type and amount of oil needed for your car and the proper oil filter/gasket. You will also need an oil filter wrench, socket set, funnel, pan for catching the old oil, gloves, safety glasses, and clothes you don't mind getting dirty. Required tools can vary depending on the make and model of the car.

Once again, I highly recommend you practice this procedure in a safe spot with someone experienced to watch over you and provide guidance.

1. Consult the manual to find the oil fill cap and drain plug's location.
2. Open the hood and remove the oil fill cap. Store it in a safe place to prevent misplacement.
3. You will most likely need to raise the front of the car to access the oil drain plug.
   ◊ If you drive a monster 4-wheel-drive truck, you should be able to wiggle your body under the vehicle to get your business done.
   ◊ For those of us who own a regular-sized car, I highly recommend using a set of auto service ramps.
      + DO NOT USE A JACK unless you have jack stands to stabilize the vehicle. Nothing will ruin your day faster than getting crushed by your car when it falls off the jack!

 **WARNING:** To avoid personal injury from burns, make sure the engine has cooled down before draining oil.

4. Carefully position yourself under the vehicle. Using the proper size socket and wrench, locate the oil drain plug and remove it quickly. To avoid an epic mess, make sure your pan is in place to catch the draining oil.

5. Inspect the oil plug and gasket and replace it if it appears to be in poor condition; otherwise, clean and reinstall the plug once the oil has drained. Ensure you do not overtighten this plug, as it can damage the threads and result in an oil leak.

6. Locate the oil filter/gasket and remove it using your oil filter wrench. Make sure your drip pan is placed directly underneath it before removing it. Dump excess oil from the old filter into the oil pan, then discard the old filter.

7. Grab your new filter and lubricate the gasket by dipping your finger into the old oil in the pan and smearing it onto the gasket.

8. Install the new oil filter and hand-tighten it. DO NOT USE OIL FILTER WRENCH to tighten the filter.

9. Carefully remove yourself from below the vehicle and get topside to the engine compartment. WATCH YOUR HEAD.

10. Grab your funnel and stick it into the oil fill tube. Crack open your first quart of new oil and dump it in.

    ◊ It is CRITICAL that you are using both the right amount and type of oil needed for your specific car.

    ◊ Be sure to replace the oil fill cap when finished.

11. Start your engine and, if applicable, back the car down off the ramps (or jack up and remove jack stands) onto level ground. Check your

oil pressure gauge for proper oil pressure reading or make sure the engine oil pressure warning light does not come on.

  ◊ Depending on the type of car, you may have to reset your oil life meter manually.

  ◊ If all is good, kill the engine and check the oil level using the steps mentioned previously to ensure you are at the appropriate level. Double-checking your work is never a bad idea!

12. Make sure to set a reminder for your next oil change. Times between changes will vary depending on the car and the type of oil you use. You guessed it: refer to your car's manual for the recommended oil change schedule.

13. Properly dispose of your used oil by pouring it into a secure container, then find a local facility to recycle it. Oil can be recycled at most auto shops that sell oil.

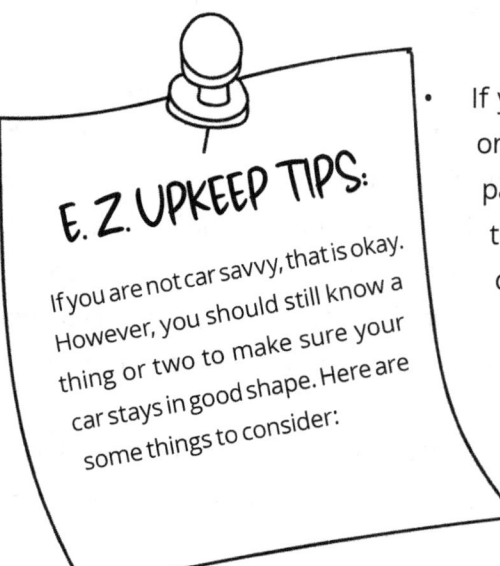

E. Z. UPKEEP TIPS:

If you are not car savvy, that is okay. However, you should still know a thing or two to make sure your car stays in good shape. Here are some things to consider:

- If your check engine light comes on, you can go to just about any car parts shop, such as AutoZone, and they will read and interpret the code for you for free.
  - ◊ The check engine light coming on isn't always something super-serious. It can turn on from something as simple as not properly screwing your gas cap back on.
  - ◊ There are many instances where the check engine light may stay on even after the problem is fixed; don't panic just yet. Sometimes the car needs to run a bit to determine that the problem is truly fixed.
- If your tire pressure warning light comes on, again, do not panic! This does not automatically mean you have a flat tire; many sensors are super-sensitive and will go off if the tire's PSI is off just a little bit.
- Read your manual and get to know your gauge cluster, as the lights and warnings can vary depending on the vehicle model, make, and year.

OH NO! CAR CRASH!

Being in a car accident is scary enough, but the steps after an accident can be scary, too, if not handled right!

Car accidents are exactly that — accidents. I imagine most people don't get in their car and think, *What a lovely day to get in a fender bender*! At least, I hope not.

Follow some basic steps after you are in an accident to help make sure the story is told correctly and you do not end up getting screwed over by a person who likes to take advantage of others' insurance.

I must note, this section was created after a student of mine was in her first car accident, and not knowing what to do was a very stressful and scary experience for her. I was asked to include this information in the book, and of course, I obliged. This is most certainly a stressful situation, and being prepared can make it a little less scary.

Here is a breakdown of the basics. Obviously, depending on the circumstances, the steps may differ.

Snap, crackle, crunch, you've been in an accident! What do you do first?

- First thing is first, you want to immediately assess the situation for safety and injuries sustained by yourself and passengers, if any.
    ◊ STAY CALM! I am aware this is easier said than done, but a calm mind tends to think more clearly, while a panicked mind is more likely to make mistakes.
    ◊ If someone is badly injured, avoid moving them if possible. Abruptly moving a person with something like a spinal cord injury can turn the injury from severe to fatal.
        + If staying in place is not an option, move them as slowly and gently as possible to a safe spot where they can stay until paramedics arrive.
    ◊ Call the police to report the accident.
        + Please note that laws regarding police involvement in an accident differ depending on where you reside. Always make sure you know your state's rules and regulations.

What to do with your car immediately after an accident.

- If you are on a busy road or highway, do not just jump out of your car immediately to check things out. That can lead to a whole different list of problems for you!
    ◊ If you are on a busy road and your car **is** drivable, slowly pull over to the side of the road and out of traffic.
    ◊ If you are on a busy road and your car **is not** drivable, stay in your car, call the police, and wait for responders to arrive and safely block off the area.

- If you are in an area with little to no traffic, you are likely safe to keep your car where it is. Either stay in your car or make sure you are standing safely off of the road.
  - ◊ Keeping the accident scene intact will give the best details for interpreting exactly what happened. However, the safety of everyone involved should take top priority, so make the decision you feel most comfortable with.

WHAT SHOULD I DO AFTER A CAR ACCIDENT?

☐ GET TO A SAFE SPOT.

☐ DO NOT LEAVE.

☐ REMAIN CALM.

☐ GET IMMEDIATE MEDICAL HELP.

☐ TAKE PICTURES

☐ ALWAYS GET A POLICE REPORT.

Get This:

☐ DATE + TIME + CONDITIONS
☐ NAMES OF THOSE INVOLVED
☐ WITNESS NAMES/ CONTACTS
☐ LICENSE PLATES OF THOSE INVOLVED
☐ LIST OF ALL DAMAGE/ INJURIES

GIVE THIS:

☐ NAME
☐ VEHICLE INFO
☐ INSURANCE INFO
☐ POLICY INFO

NEVER leave the scene of an accident until all the proper steps have been completed.

- Keep in mind that some people will flee the scene, if possible, to avoid having any financial responsibility, getting in trouble, etc. Try to be aware of the other parties involved and their actions.
- Keep a pen and paper nearby to write down the license plate number and car description ASAP. You can also get your phone out to record and take pictures of the car. Then if the other party flees, you have a better chance of finding them.

Document, document, DOCUMENT!

- This is one of the main reasons you keep your insurance card in your glove box. It is nice to have it easily accessible and ready to use.
  - ◊ You will want to exchange insurance information with other parties involved. Make sure you write down their name, insurance company name, policy number, and card details.
    - + You can also snap pictures of the front and back of the card.
- If it is safe to do so, get as many pictures and videos of the scene and the involved vehicles as you can, especially if the accident is not your fault.
- When you are in an accident, your adrenaline is running high and it can be hard to recall exact details later on, so documenting as much as possible will be a big help, especially if things get sketchy with insurances and different parties' sides of the story.

Important details to document:

- The date, time, location, and weather/road conditions of the accident.
- Damage to your vehicle and any others involved.
- A picture or video of the entire scene to see how and where the impact occurred.
- Make, model, license plate numbers of other vehicles involved.
- Details regarding any injuries sustained by everyone involved.

Working with the emergency responders:

- One party should call the police and paramedics as quickly after the accident happens as possible. It is okay if more than one person calls; better safe than sorry!
    - ◊ Again, this is not legally necessary in all states, but it can be another layer of protection if you are not the one at fault and having issues with the insurance claim.
- Most importantly, if there are any injuries, those should be addressed and taken care of first.
- Work with the police to write an official report that you will use later when working with insurance companies to settle your claim.

How to handle filing an insurance claim after an accident:

- You will want to call *your* insurance company as soon as possible after the accident to create and open a claim.

VEHICULAR VOCABULARY

Every car is smart when it has a smart driver!

Here are some common vehicle-related terms you may come across from time to time. Learn them.

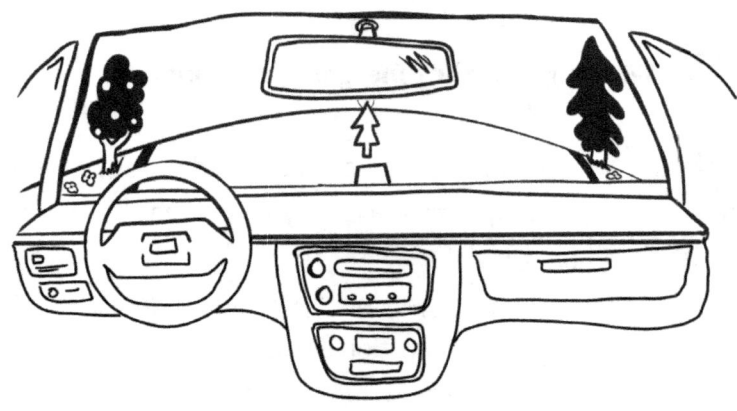

AWD: All-wheel drive

ABS: Anti-lock braking system

ACC: Adaptive cruise control

DRL: Daytime running lights (or lamps)

FWD: Front-wheel drive

HP: Horsepower

RPM: Revolutions per minute

RWD: Rear-wheel drive

SUV: Sport utility vehicle

TCS: Traction control system

VIN: Vehicle identification number

4WD: Four-wheel drive

DASHBOARD WARNING
LIGHTS + MEANINGS

 Turn Signals

 High Beam Light

 Anti-Lock Break Sys

 Warning Light

 Master Lighting

 Slip Indicator

 Windshield Defrost

 Child Safety Locks

 Glow Plug (Diesel)

 All-Wheel Drive

 Overdrive Indicator

 Engine Management

 Tire Pressure

 Rear Window Defrost

 Cruise Control

 Powertrain

 Electronic Stability

 Low Fuel Notification

 Fog Beams Indicator

 Brake System Alert

 Front Airbag

 Open Doors

 Oil Pressure Warning

 Seat Belt Reminder

 Temperature Warning

 Battery Warning

 Hazard Warning Lights

OBTAINING & MAINTAINING A SWEET RIDE POP QUIZ!

Who doesn't love a pop quiz? Especially one where there are no wrong answers?!

Read each question and really take the time to ponder the answers — not how you *THINK* you should answer, but how you *WANT* to answer! Use the blank space below to write down your answers or anything you'd like. It is your book, after all!

E. Z. TIP:

To make this book personal to your life, write down your answers in the area provided and leave yourself some space to revamp your responses as you experience the different twists and turns of your adulting journey.

QUIZ QUESTIONS

1. What type of vehicle do you feel will best suit your lifestyle? Think about the type of terrain you plan to drive on, what type of gas mileage you want, if you plan to haul things or not, and of course, what fits into your budget.

2. What features are important that you have in your car? Make a list of things that are your "must-haves" and your "wants, not needs." Keep the list on you when shopping for a vehicle so you stay on the right track.

3. Can't decide between a few different models? Use the handy chart below to help you compare and contrast your top choices.

Use this space to start planning out your journey to adulting happiness!

Make	Model/Trim	Mileage

Price	Pros	Cons

CHILLIN' IN YOUR CRIB

DON'T END UP LIVING IN A VAN DOWN BY THE RIVER...
UNLESS THAT IS YOUR GOAL...

In case you were not aware, choosing your preferred shelter option is a majorly essential and adult decision to make. Sheltering safely is one of the four basic needs of human survival, right next to air, water, and food. Trust me when I tell you that you will want to find a living situation you love, a place where you feel safe and happy.

Your shelter should be your sanctuary, which can look many different ways for different people. This chapter is bursting full of things to learn and consider when it comes time to make your own living arrangements. Enjoy this little tale I have to tell, then get ready to learn!

By this point, you probably have a general idea of the kind of person I am: weird, goofy, blunt, and stubborn, just to name a few adjectives. This chapter's little anecdote really highlights my stubborn side nicely!

E. Z. DID IT!

I've always been the kind of person who enjoys "teasing" myself by looking up different big goals I want for myself and my future at some point: a lake house, an old-body American muscle car, a personal chef, etc. Some goals may be more far-fetched than others. Aim for the stars, I say!

In my later teenage years, I was all about researching different home options available in my area, trying to decide where I desired to see myself living when it was time to fly the family nest. I planted the idea in my head that I *had* to own a place. Renting always seemed like a waste of money to me, and I wanted to have total control over my own dwelling. I may have forgotten to mention my OCD and slight control issues in my earlier self-description, two traits that have been both a blessing and a curse throughout my life.

When I decided the right option for me was to buy my own place, I had to determine what type of home I wanted to buy. It didn't take long to fall in love with the idea of living the condo life: no yard to maintain, and it is set up like an apartment, but I own everything and have complete creative freedom (insert evil laugh here). For me, it was a no-brainer.

Fast-forward to my 21st year of life: I had my first adult job with benefits, and my wings were getting itchy and twitchy. I was ready to fly the coop and be on my own. In typical Erica fashion, I researched the home-buying process for hours on end until I felt comfortable understanding what my next steps needed to be.

Once I had drafted a game plan and a clear vision, I hit the ground running at a full-on sprint. Within a few weeks, I connected with a lovely real estate agent I happen to be related to. She helped me get approved for a loan, answered all my questions, and set me up with an online portal to keep track of properties I was interested in. Soon after, we set up a time to view the condos that piqued my interest, and when I walked into the third (or fourth) condo on my list, I felt like I had walked into my home. It just felt right. They say, "when you know, you know," and I knew that I knew, so I wasted no time and submitted my offer.

I should probably note that during the couple of weeks that all of this was happening, my parents were on a different continent, and communication was rather sparse. My email correspondence to the folks went a little something like this:

Me: *Hey Mom & Dad! How's Germany treating you? Guess what? I found a home loan lender, filled out all the paperwork and such, and I was officially approved for a loan the other day! Take care and have fun! K bye.*

Me: *Hiya Folks! Heading out later to look at a couple of condos that look interesting; I am just excited to look around and see some options. I won't make any big decisions without you, and we can look together when you are back home. Auf Wiedersehen!*

Me: *Oh, hey lovely parents of mine! Soooooo... I found a condo that I am in love with. I mean, it is perfect for me, AND it is only a couple of miles away from you! Doesn't that sound great? I hope so because I put an offer on it! I should hear back right around when you will be coming back home. I promise not to accept or sign anything until you check the place out and give me your thoughts. Gute reise meine lieben eltern!*

I will be the first to admit that was probably not the correct way to make such a critical adulting decision. I never expected to find my dream condo and for the home-buying process to go as quickly as it did. Please note, however, that while this process seemingly flew by, that does NOT mean it wasn't full of stressful, anxiety-inducing decisions by any means!

I have lived in my place for over 12 years now, and for the most part, it has been great. I still love my unit, the location, and the setting; what I do not love is my Homeowner's Association (HOA) fee that has tripled over the years and the complex's elected board, whose motives have always seemed a bit too sketchy. At 21, I wasn't thinking about looking into the board's operations, talking to other owners about their thoughts on the complex, or taking the time to understand precisely how a condo complex operates.

You live, and you learn, for that is how you grow and evolve, if you ask me!

WHAT'S IN IT FOR YOU!

When you rush into things and become blinded by all the shiny, exciting possibilities, it is easy to overlook important things. Fear not, though, for some of the more confusing-sounding terms I have used throughout this magical tale will be explained in detail later in this chapter. This information will help guide you to make the right choice for you.

Whether you want to rent or own, doing your research and starting your home hunt when you feel adequately educated and prepared is the best way to go, in my humble opinion at least. When you buy or rent a place of your own, you are moving into the community and environment as well, so making sure you are happy with those details is every bit as important as being happy with your new home. Take your time, do your research, and ask as many questions as your heart desires; you will be just fine!

I can tell you when it comes time for me to move, I will be rereading this chapter and taking my own advice for sure!

RENTING A PLACE

Rented or not, you deserve a safe space to call your own!

Before you start looking for an apartment or house to rent, review your budget to figure out what you can afford either by yourself or with a roommate. Decide what neighborhood you would like to live in. Think about the amenities you want, such as parking, which floor you'd like to live on (if you live on an upper floor, is there an elevator or only stairs?), pool/gym, washer and dryer access, pet-friendly, etc. I suggest you do this before you start looking into your rental options. It is always nice to be prepared and approach big decisions such as this with a game plan.

Give yourself time to search for the right place so you are not feeling rushed; also, keep in mind that rent prices can change based on the season. Before signing a lease, update your budget to include future housing expenses and any other upfront costs you may be responsible for. Don't sign anything if you cannot afford it.

Don't forget to ask what utilities you will need to pay to include in your budget. Get together paperwork you may need to submit along with the rental application (i.e., credit score, rental history, proof of income, personal references, etc.). Create a list of furnishings you have or need, and be organized and prepared for move-in day. Don't be afraid to ask the property manager as many questions as you want. This is a BIG deal!

BUYING A HOME

They say home is where the heart is; make sure you buy
a place you love!

Here are some points to consider before you take the plunge into the wonderful world of homeownership.

- **Do your research:** Research homes in the area you are interested in, **watch listings**, pay attention to how long they have been on the market (for sale), how their prices have changed, etc. Doing this will help give you a sense of **market trends** in that area.

> **Watching Listings**: Searching for any type of home to rent or own is a fairly easy task, thanks to multiple different apps that draw their data from the Multiple Listing Service (MLS). Real estate brokers and agents own and operate the MLS, making it the country's most accurate, comprehensive, and powerful system.
> - Popular house-hunting companies such as Zillow, Trulia, Homesnap, and Redfin make it easy for you to search exactly what type of property you are looking for, your price range, the area you want to live in, desired home features, and more. Users can typically make an account through these apps to save their search parameters and be notified when a new property hits the market.

◊ Keep in mind, a house that has been on the market for a long time, or taken off and put back on the market several times, likely has a negative reason behind it, such as being overpriced or major damage needing to be repaired.

• **What can you afford?** Determine how much of a house payment you can afford. Lenders suggest you look for homes that cost no more than three to five times your annual income, though you need to take your present debt/financial situation into account as well when deciding what you can afford.

Market Trends: These are patterns and changes in the real estate market that are significant enough to cause a statistical change.

◊ Get prequalified and preapproved with a lender before looking at homes. Getting prequalified for a mortgage will let you know exactly how much you have to spend on a home.

◊ Make sure you select the right type of loan for you. The many different types of loans come with their own pros and cons. Do your research and pick the one that works best for your situation.

◊ Offering a higher down payment percentage can tell the owner that you are serious about wanting to buy their home, making it that much more appealing to work with you. This option is not feasible for all home buyers, and there's nothing wrong with that. Here are some things to consider regarding your down payment:

  + The average down payment percentages can greatly differ depending on factors such as the state you are buying in, whether you are a first-time home buyer, or any type of loan or program you may qualify for.

  + Being able to put down a 20% payment on a home can have benefits such as not having to pay any private mortgage insurance (PMI) on your loan.

- **Find the right real estate agent:** Find an agent who is knowledgeable about the area you want to move to and with whom you have a good connection. A well-seasoned agent can save you both money and frustrations.

- **House hunting:** Take your time, find a home you love, and then make an offer. You should never settle in any facet of life that can compromise your happiness. Homeownership is most definitely one of those facets.

  ◊ You will likely look at a lot of houses, so keep notes and take pictures to remember details about each place.

◊ Make sure you test electric, plumbing, open doors/windows, etc.

- **Get the home inspected:** It is critical to have a thorough **home inspection** done to ensure there are no significant issues with the house that will cost you a ton of money.
    - ◊ Having certain issues fixed may be **negotiated into the contract** for the seller to repair before purchase. Don't be afraid to advocate for yourself where this topic is concerned. It can save you a lot of future stress and money!
    - ◊ If the home inspection reveals too many problems, you can also back out of a contract.

Home Inspection: Having your potential new home thoroughly checked over before you decide to take the next steps toward purchasing is important for several reasons.

- Lenders may not finance your loan without the home being inspected first.
- A thorough home inspection can uncover major problems that could be both costly and dangerous, such as issues with faulty wiring, mold, plumbing, the foundation, roofing, and more.
    - ◊ Serious issues such as these can be easily overlooked by potential buyers simply because they don't know what to look for, whereas a professional inspection should cover the finer, less obvious aspects of the home.
- Skipping this step in the home-buying process could end up landing you in serious financial trouble, potentially to the point where you could be forced into foreclosure.

Negotiate into the Contract: When buying a home, you are not obligated to pay the exact amount the seller is asking for. Unless there is a major real estate boom happening, being smart about crafting an offer on the home you pick can save you both money and frustration. Keep in mind, negotiations don't necessarily have to be monetary. The following are some things to consider before you put in an offer on your dream home.

- First, while most buyers hope to pay below asking price for the home they want, you need to make sure the offer you submit isn't so low that the seller feels like you are wasting their time, causing them to reject your offer and be uninterested in further negotiations.
- It is possible to ask the seller to pay upfront costs associated with the home-buying process, such as closing, inspection, and warranty fees.
  - ◊ On the other side of this, if you are financially capable enough to offer to take on some or all of these costs, it can make your offer more appealing to the seller.
- Depending on what is found during the home inspection, you can negotiate to have the seller fix the repairs before closing or cover costs by lowering your final offer.
- You can try to negotiate to keep certain appliances, fixtures, and furniture in the contract.
- Being flexible with your closing/possession date can work to your benefit, especially if the seller needs or wants to be out at a specific time.

- **Have the home appraised:** Usually, the lender will arrange to have the home appraised to determine the current fair market value on the property; this way, all parties will know if you are paying a fair price.
  - ◊ Make sure you double-check with all parties to determine who is responsible for setting up the home appraisal. You do not want to skip this step.
- **Close the sale:** If all the points above have been considered and you still feel like this is the home for you, you will move forward with the purchasing process. A set closing date will be set on the home when ownership will officially be transferred from the seller to the buyer.
  - ◊ At the closing, you will sign all the paperwork to complete the sale and get your loan (SO. MUCH. PAPERWORK.). Once the closing is complete, you will be ready to move into your new home!

E. Z. TIP:

When settling into your new dwelling, make sure you learn the maintenance and upkeep requirements for your appliances and such: things like cleaning vents, washer/dryer upkeep, changing the air filters every few months in your furnace, etc. Keep up on these things from the start. It's much cheaper to maintain your home than pay for repairs if anything breaks.

THINGS TO THINK ABOUT BEFORE YOU MOVE IN

The keyword here is BEFORE!

Renting or purchasing a place to call home is a HUGE deal, and it can be easy to overlook things and rush into a major decision. The following are good questions to ask yourself before signing a contract of any kind:

- **What are the crime rates in the area?**
  - ◊ Search crime rate statistics and crimes that have happened in that specific area in the last five to 10 years. Are crime rates dropping or rising?
- **Is the area considered a flood plain?**
  - ◊ Keep in mind that many insurance companies will not cover flood damage costs in these areas.
- **Does the neighborhood have an HOA fee?**
  - ◊ If so, what is the cost, when is it due, and what does it cover?
- **What are the neighborhood rules?**
  - ◊ For example, pet limits, street parking rules, landscaping rules, etc.
- **When were major repairs/replacements made last?**
  - ◊ For example, roof, air conditioner, furnace, appliances, etc.

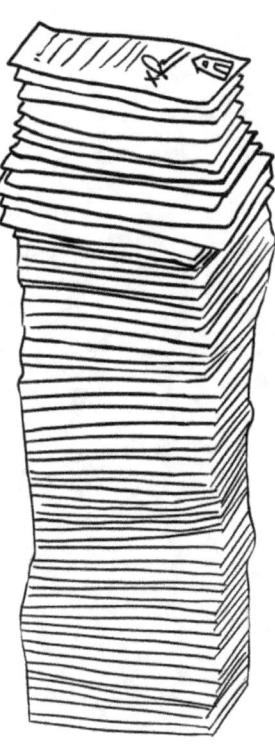

- **Are the other houses in the neighborhood well maintained?**
- **Do you prefer a home that runs on gas, electric, or both?**
- **Do you plan on potentially raising kids there?**
  - ◊ If so, is the school district desirable?
- **What are the school ratings?**
- **Is the traffic in the area heavy or too much?**
  - ◊ Are there noises you are okay with hearing nonstop, such as traffic noises, trains, and planes?
- **What is the parking situation?**
- **Are the roads well maintained?**
- **What convenient locations would you like to live closer to?**
  - ◊ For example, certain stores, highways, entertainment, farmers' markets, etc.

IS THAT ROOMIE RIGHT FOR YOU?

Living with somebody is a solid way to figure out if a person is a friend or foe!

Moving into a new home is exciting, and living with a roommate (or several) can be great to help save money and a lot of fun if you pick the right person to live with. However, you need to keep in mind that just because you are best friends with a person, that does NOT mean you will be compatible roommates!

Ask yourself these questions *BEFORE* committing to living with somebody:

- Do you prefer to live with someone who is excessively clean? Can you handle somebody who is messy?
- Do you care if a roommate comes with a pet? Do you have or want a pet?
  - ◊ If you answered yes to either of these, are you moving somewhere pet-friendly?
- Does it matter how long guests stay and how often?
- Are parties allowed, and if so, how big and how late? How does your potential roommate feel about parties?

- ◊ Setting boundaries you agree on beforehand can save future stress and confrontation!
- Whose name will the utilities be under?
- How will you collect or give rent, utility, grocery, etc., payments?
  - ◊ Coming up with a payment plan/schedule before moving in is another great idea to implement to avoid future issues.
- Who will buy the furniture and take it with them if someone moves out?
- How do you pay the rent to the landlord? Or the mortgage payment if one of you owns the home?
  - ◊ When is it due?
  - ◊ Are there late fees?
- Under what circumstances can your landlord or other "strangers" enter your place without you being home or giving you notice?
- Are there penalties for breaking your lease agreement early if you need to?
- How do your schedules mix? Any conflicts?
- Any habits that are roommate deal-breakers?
  - ◊ For example, smoking, being loud, unorganized, up too late or early, etc.

If you decide to rent a place with a roommate, make sure you BOTH sign the lease so someone isn't left screwed over if something happens and somebody needs or wants to move out sooner than planned.

CHILLIN' IN YOUR CRIB POP QUIZ!

Great news! No quiz for this chapter... mainly because the last two sections are essentially a test! Plus, I want to leave you enough note space to answer the questions that matter the most to you! You're welcome!

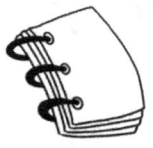

Use this space to start planning out your journey to adulting happiness!

_____

_____

_____

_____

_____

_____

_____

_____

_____

_____

_____

_____

_____

_____

_____

TREAT YO-SELF

TAKE THE TIME TO TAKE CARE OF
YOURSELF: MIND, BODY, AND SOUL.

When you feel truly happy and content in your life, it is a feeling like no other. Achieving that mind and body balance of peace is not always easy, and it requires you to continually put in the work within yourself. Part of putting in that work involves trusting medical professionals to make sure you journey through life happily and healthily. Another big part requires you to educate and advocate for yourself.

There will be times that you feel like getting to this point is impossible, but know you are not alone, and you will pull through it as a better person on the other side. This chapter provides information for you to understand and utilize to ensure you are taking care of yourself the way you deserve to be cared for, including understanding the different types of doctors available to you to ensure you get yourself the proper care, how to protect yourself from predators, how to find your mental health happy place, and more.

E. Z. DID IT!

What exactly does "treat yo-self" really mean? That is a great question and one I can only answer for myself. To me, "treat yo-self" can include everything from having homemade waffles and ice cream for dinner to staying in my jammies all day relaxing to kicking it into beast mode and exercising like a wild woman, sweating out all my frustrations. It also means being attuned to my own mental and physical needs, and recognizing when it is time to make a doctor's appointment. What works for me doesn't work for everyone, which is completely fine. In the scheme of things, it only has to work for me!

Those who know me know that I love to unwind by slapping on my sweatpants and watching scary movies for hours, and many people don't understand how I can find that enjoyable. You know what, though? They don't have to. I love it, and that is what counts.

I love turning on a horror movie after a long, stressful day. Things might have been rough that day, but at least nobody chased me through a forest with a machete, so I count it as a victory. It puts things weirdly into perspective for me and allows me to realize that things could be much, much worse! The doctor prescribed medications I am on to help me stay positive and focused on the world around me when sweatpants and movies aren't available.

When you are *booted* into the world of adulting, you will begin experiencing freedom on a whole new level — a freedom that will allow you to truly understand what your body and mind need to stay in a healthy place. There is no cookie-cutter cure-all for this; I believe a person's genetics and environmental factors play a crucial role in determining the best way to treat oneself.

I also think that you should never let a person, or societal norms, pressure you into feeling or acting some type of way. Let's shine that spotlight back over to me for a second. I am a 30-something, very happily single and childless, independent woman. If I were alive in the 1600s through the 1800s, I have no doubt I would have been called a witch and burned at the stake! So, I am grateful to live in a time when a woman can be independent and not automatically labeled as a pariah; all of my pets help with that label enough.

Don't get me wrong; I still deal with people who constantly ask me if I am dating somebody, with that tone in their voices that leads me to believe they feel bad for me being a single woman, like it wasn't my conscious choice for a reason. As if being in a relationship and wanting to pop out 1.93 children is the key to a woman leading a full, satisfying life. It is a satisfying life for many people, though, and nothing is wrong with that.

If you fall asleep each night feeling content about yourself and your situation, that is all that matters, if you ask me. If you lay your head down on your pillow feeling like something is missing, then you need to think about what you need to do to fill that void in a healthy, safe manner, whether it be through natural or medicinal routes.

Do not wait until that feeling starts to consume every facet of your life to the point you feel as if you may explode. That is not a place where you are likely to make the best decisions for yourself.

WHAT'S IN IT FOR YOU!

Mental health has always been a taboo and touchy subject; I would even dare to categorize it with conversation topics regarding politics and religion. How did we get to a place where expressing our innermost thoughts and feelings became something that people were ashamed of? News flash: life is not all cupcakes and kittens (two of my favorite things, FYI). Nobody leads a perfect, carefree life; if they say they do, they are lying.

You are the one who will know yourself and your needs better than anybody else, and you are also the one who will be your best advocate at the end of the day. If you don't self-advocate and voice your needs or wants, do you think anybody else will? Maybe, maybe not. As you go through life, you will start learning a lot about yourself, including the type of person you are, were, or want to become.

Listen to that inner voice and do what you must to keep yourself feeling sane. Talk to a mental healthcare specialist. Try medications if you genuinely think they will help and are the right thing for you. Do hot yoga in a smoky, incense-filled room. Cut out toxic people in your life. I believe people come into your life for a purpose; that purpose does not always need to include a lifelong connection. Do YOU!

Bear with me while I try not to sound too much like a complete greeting card cliché, but if you do not love yourself and the kind of person you view yourself as, why would you expect others to feel that way about you?

If I can preach about one thing I am beginning to learn I am great at regarding my adulting journey, it is self-love. The more I learn about myself, the more I realize what makes me happy and that there is so much I can do on my own to feel grateful for the life I lead: a road trip with a best friend, floating in the pool with my family, exploring creeks and parks hunting for unique, shiny rocks. I know how to have a good time by my own personally bedazzled definition!

As you travel through life, you will learn that too. Never apologize for treating yo-self and putting your needs first sometimes. I don't care what anybody says; you will never adequately care for other people if you can't take care of yourself. I will end my self-love, "do you" rant here and leave you to enjoy this chapter all about different ways to concoct your own "treat yo-self" definition!

PHYSICAL HEALTH CARE

Finding the right doctor is of primary importance!

Part of adulting is taking charge of your health and needs, including full-body health, eye, dental, and specialty care. First things first: FIND DOCTORS YOU LIKE AND TRUST!

I suggest using the information in this chapter to aid you in your quest to find the perfect physician for you.

Just because a person is a doctor does not mean they are always right or always have your best interests in mind. If you go to an appointment and leave feeling uneasy about the doctor, keep looking until you find the right fit. You only get this one body, so treat it right!

Before finding a doctor or medical care facility, you MUST make sure they accept your health insurance. When you make an appointment, DOUBLE-CHECK that they take your insurance and figure out what is covered and what you will be expected to pay up front so you don't end up with a surprise giant bill.

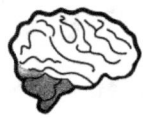

TYPES OF DOCTORS & MEDICAL SPECIALTIES:

- **Primary care physician or primary care provider (PCP):** This is your main doctor, the one you will see for your yearly physical exams and appointments for any issues you are having.
  - ◊ Typically, your primary care doctor will connect you with any type of specialty doctors/care you may need and will guide you through your healthcare journey.
  - ◊ Find a primary care doctor you trust with your life and who you truly feel has your best interests in mind!
- **Nurse practitioner or physician's assistant:** These are medical professionals trained to provide patients with basic, nonemergent care.
  - ◊ For more routine office visits, you may see one of these types of medical professionals rather than your primary physician.
- **Internal medicine doctor (internist):** These doctors usually only see adult patients. They provide primary care as well as the diagnosis and treatment of many more serious medical maladies.
- **Family medicine doctor:** This is a doctor that will see both adult and child patients. They practice preventive medicine as well as manage various medical conditions.
- **Pediatrician:** These doctors treat infants, children, and teenage patients. They provide basic medical care and the treatment and diagnosis of medical issues, especially those pertaining to behavioral and physical developments associated with their young patients.

- **Cardiologist:** Specialist dealing with the heart and circulatory system.
- **Dermatologist:** Specialist dealing with skin, hair, and nails, who you would see to get moles and such checked.
    - ◊ Having your body checked regularly for mole and skin abnormalities is very important, especially depending on factors such as genetics and time spent in the sun. Skin cancer is very real and very deadly.
- **Endocrinologist:** Specialist dealing with hormones and metabolism.
- **Gastroenterologist:** Specialist dealing with digestive organs: stomach, liver, gallbladder, pancreas, bowels, etc.
- **Neurologist:** Specialist dealing with the nervous system: brain, nerves, spinal cord.
- **Obstetrician/gynecologist (OB/GYN):** Specialist focusing on women's health: Pap smears, pregnancy, childbirth, pelvic exams, etc.
- **Oncologist:** Specialist that deals with cancers and their treatment.
- **Ophthalmologist:** Specialist dealing with eyes.
- **Otorhinolaryngologist (aka ENT):** Specialist that deals with medical needs of the head and neck.
    - ◊ ENT = Ears, Nose, Throat
- **Pathologist:** Specialist dealing with diagnosing different issues through microscopic examinations of bodily tissues.
- **Podiatrist:** Specialist dealing with your ankles and feet.
- **Pulmonologist:** Specialist dealing with breathing issues.
- **Rheumatologist:** Specialist dealing with issues involving joints, bones, muscles, and tendons.
- **Sports medicine physician:** Specialist dealing with sports/exercise injuries.
- **Urologist:** Specialist dealing with the urinary tract; they also see males for prostate exams and infertility issues.

MENTAL HEALTH CARE

Make sure you take the time to take care of your mind!

Mental illness includes a large variety of conditions that affect a person's behavior, thought processes, and mood. Common mental disorders in young adults include anxiety, depression, panic attacks, PTSD, and other mood-altering challenges.

Keep these E. Z. tips in mind when evaluating your mental health status:

- Never let anybody tell you or make you feel like something is wrong with you. By anybody, I am essentially referring to people who fall outside of your family, friends, and medical circle.
- Don't allow a stranger's snap judgments make you feel "less than." Being able to recognize and admit you need help is an important step in your journey to happiness.
- Be confident with your own identity; understand that it is okay to feel off and reach out for help. Admitting that you need help and then finding your own care is a very empowering feeling.
- You are going through a huge transition into adulthood. Or maybe you have been in the world of adulting for a while now, and the struggle is real. Plain and simple. It's okay to be anxious and stressed.
- You will go through difficult times in your life, and you will experience rejection and failure. Everyone does. What everyone does not do, though, is cope in a healthy manner when things go wrong. Learn to cope healthily!
- NOBODY can change you except YOU!

- Your emotions and thoughts are just that — *yours*. They are your emotions to control; don't let others take charge of *your* emotions and *your* thoughts.
- If you feel certain ways you don't see displayed among your loved ones or portrayed in characters you watch on television, that is okay. It should never make you feel any less validated.
- If you feel like you have to conceal your true self around certain people, consider taking a step back to think about the reasons for this. Pretending to be somebody you're not to placate others is exhausting!
- Learn to love yourself first, and then surround yourself with people who love you for you, weird quirks and all. It is not an easy feat by any means, especially while busting out into the adulting lifestyle for the first time, but I promise you, it is worth the work and effort. Any time somebody calls me "weird," I embrace it and let them know I think normal is boring! What is "normal," really?

I sincerely hope the information in this chapter makes that journey a little easier for you!

Signs that you are likely struggling with your mental health include:

- Difficulty sleeping and feeling tired all the time
- Quickly going from hyperactivity to exhaustion (going from 100 to 0)
- Losing interest in the things you typically love
- Feeling worried or scared all the time
- Not wanting to hang out and participate in activities with your friends and family
- Extreme mood swings: high highs, and low lows
- Having suicidal thoughts
- Issues with focusing and completing everyday tasks
- Constant feelings of negativity, sadness, or being overwhelmed
- Crabby or feeling irritated constantly
- Weight gain or weight loss (eating more or eating less)

Natural ways to cope with mental health struggles:

Maybe you don't like doctors. Maybe you have crummy health insurance options. Maybe there's another reason that is nobody's business but your own. That does not mean you cannot and should not be able to cope with your feelings in appropriate, healthy ways.

Free, cheap &
natural self-care
coping mechanism
ideas:

- Exercise! Whether it be joining a gym, hiking, or a stroll around the block, get that heart rate up and that dopamine pumping. It can be hard to motivate yourself to exercise, but you won't regret it. Sweat out your frustrations!
- Watch upbeat and uplifting things on television, not horror and true crime stuff... unless that is what works for you. Watch what *you* want to!
- Get lost in a good book.
- Clean and organize your space; donate unwanted items to help those in need.

- VENT, SCREAM, CRY!
- Handle the problems as they come; do not bottle them up until you explode!
- Zone out to your favorite music or learn how to play an instrument and jam out to music you create yourself!
- Get a pet to care for if you have the means to do so.
  - ◊ Please keep in mind, taking on a pet family member is a HUGE responsibility. If you decide to get an animal, make sure you do the proper research to find the right pet for you. Also, make

sure you have the financial and living situation that can support that animal for its entire life. Do NOT get a pet as a way to try and fix your mental health state. If careful consideration is not taken, this could land you in a worse mindset than you were before.

- Volunteer at an animal shelter as a dog walker or volunteer at any organization that interests you.
- Find a hobby you enjoy: coloring, cooking, rock hunting, origami, diamond painting, sports, etc.
- Eat healthily and take proper vitamins and supplements.
- Experiment with different essential oils.
- Talk to somebody, someone you know well or a medical professional, about your feelings.
- Sit outside; get some fresh air and sunlight.
- Keep a journal and write about the things that make you happy, what you love about yourself, and long-term and short-term goals — things you can read and smile about when you are having a rough time.

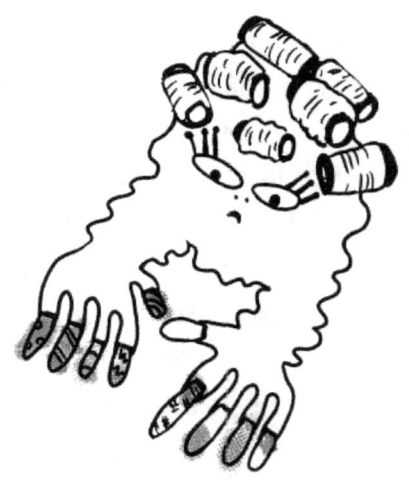

SEEKING PROFESSIONAL HELP

There is nothing wrong with admitting that you need help, especially where mental health is concerned. You get one life, and you should live it the way you want — within legal boundaries, of course. Do not be afraid to put yourself and your happiness first sometimes.

If you are struggling with your mental health and natural efforts aren't working, another step would be to seek professional help. When it comes to the professional, make sure you are seeing somebody who can help you the way you want to be helped.

The following is a list of professionals in the mental health field. Make sure you do the research to find the appropriate type of therapy for your situation.

- **Psychiatric nurse:** A nurse who works under doctor supervision, specializes in mental health, and can help you work through your struggles with a combination of therapy and medication.
- **Psychiatrist:** A person who can diagnose and treat a variety of mental health concerns through medical exams, lab diagnostics, and medications.
- **Psychoanalyst:** A person who helps people deal with their mental health issues by using different theories and practices developed over time. They help you discover the root of your problems by guiding you through things you may have **unconsciously repressed**.
  - ◊ Be careful! Psychoanalysts do not need to have any official credentials; anyone can call themselves this!

Unconsciously Repressed: This is what happens when a person's subconscious blocks out memories, emotions, and impulses associated with an unpleasant event that causes them to feel sad, anxious, scared, or guilty.

- **Psychologist:** A person who will help talk you through any issues you may be going through.
  - ◊ They are more of a counselor and typically cannot prescribe medications.
- **Psychotherapist:** A person who uses talk therapy to work through the challenges you are dealing with, and they will help you learn more about why you are having those thoughts, behaviors, and feelings, and then work to help you overcome them.
  - ◊ This type typically combines talk therapy and medicinal therapy to help you work through mental illness struggles such as trauma, loss, depression, anxiety, and more.

DIFFERENT THERAPY TYPES

The following are common therapies that are presently being used by the medical professionals discussed above to help people overcome their mental health struggles.

Cognitive behavior therapy: With this type of therapy, you will talk with a professional about the different problems you are experiencing, and they will help you overcome these struggles by working with you on changing your mindset. They do this by teaching useful skills that you can apply to your everyday life, such as proper coping strategies, how to handle or avoid triggering situations, and how to best control your emotional and physical feelings. This type of therapy is popular for those who struggle with depression and anxiety.

Group therapy: This is a form of therapy that you would attend with a group of people battling with the same type of challenges; examples include problems with addiction, illness, and loss. Everyone shares their personal struggles with the group while a therapist guides the discussion and provides everyone with a safe space to open up in. This type of therapy can provide you with feelings of belonging and understanding that you are not the only one struggling with those problems. This style of therapy promotes positive social skills and self-growth; it can also empower you to speak up and advocate for yourself in both the therapy sessions and real life.

Exposure therapy: This therapy practice is mainly used to treat conditions such as obsessive compulsive disorder (OCD), post-traumatic stress disorder (PTSD), and different types of phobias. Through exposure therapy, you will work with your medical care specialist to identify your triggers and then expose you to them in a controlled environment. From there, you will work together to learn what practices work best for you to be able to cope in a healthy manner when exposed to those triggers in your regular, everyday life routine.

National Alliance on Mental Illness (NAMI): To continue learning about different types of mental health struggles, treatment options, and much more, head over to this organization's site. It is a great tool for you to better self-educate in order to best self-advocate.

nami.org

SELF-ADVOCATING & EDUCATING FOR YOUR HEALTH

If you don't take care of your body and mind, who will?

Self-advocacy is such an important tool in life, especially regarding things that directly affect your body or mind, such as health care. Here are some tips on ways you can make sure you are doing what you feel is right and what you are comfortable with.

- At medical appointments, ask questions, be polite yet firm, and keep the tone of the conversation respectful.
    - ◊ Ask the doctor why they think that plan is the best option for you, what results you want to see, and what possible adverse reactions could happen with this treatment.
- If you are unsure about a treatment plan your doctor gives you, you do not have to say yes, but also, you do not have to say no, especially if "confrontation" is not your strong suit.
    - ◊ You can politely say that you want to take some time to make sure you fully understand the plan and that you will make a follow-up appointment once you feel comfortable with your own understanding of it all.

◊ Whether you decide to book that follow-up and go along with the treatment plan is up to you. Either way, this approach shouldn't make anyone feel uncomfortable, and it wraps up your appointment in a positive manner.

◊ Practice the art of politely declining offers that you are unsure of or uncomfortable with. That trick can come in handy in many aspects of life!

• The relationship between you and your doctor should feel more like a partnership, where the two of you work together as a team to come up with the best course of treatment. If you feel that the relationship between you and your doctor is more of a dictatorship, it is probably time to start looking for a new one.

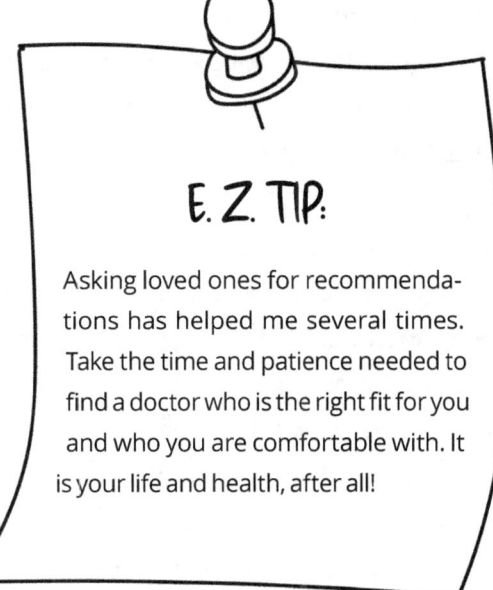

E. Z. TIP:

Asking loved ones for recommendations has helped me several times. Take the time and patience needed to find a doctor who is the right fit for you and who you are comfortable with. It is your life and health, after all!

DOCTOR *DATING*

I like to think of finding the right doctor for my needs as a little bit like dating. Doctor dating, if you will. Dare I say, doctor dating is a bit more serious though, as you are literally looking for someone you trust with your health and your life. Use these handy tips to help you find and choose the perfect doctor for you.

One more thing: While these steps should work for finding most types of doctors, it is extremely important that you follow these steps when finding your primary physician. Your primary is who you will see for general checkups and health issues. They will also have referral recommendations to specialty doctors if you need extra care. The proper primary physician is crucial!

- The first step I like to start with is writing a list of things I would like in my new doctor, things such as age, sex, type, and location.
  - ◊ I don't know about you, but I am not a fan of driving too far to a doctor's appointment when I am sick. However, if I discovered my dream doctor was just a bit further away, I would make the drive. Your health is important!
  - ◊ If you have a preexisting medical condition, it would be a good idea to find a doctor who has experience working with patients with that medical malady.
- Once you've got an idea on your dream doctor, I strongly encourage asking loved ones for recommendations. It makes me feel

better when people I know and trust are seeing a doctor they know and trust.

- ◊ Remember to still go in with an open mind; just because your loved one sees this doctor doesn't guarantee they are the right fit for you.
- ◊ You do not have to do this; you can research doctors on your own through the internet.
- ◊ Keep in mind, some doctors may not be accepting new patients at that time; it's not uncommon. This is a reason for you to make a list with several options.

- Make a list of potential doctors, get your medical insurance information handy, and make sure that doctor's office takes your specific coverage.

- ◊ You can call the office directly and ask, or most insurance companies have a website where you can search for doctors that take that coverage.
- ◊ If you do not do this step, you could end up with a MASSIVE medical bill!

- Make an appointment, meet the doctor, and trust your gut. If you don't feel like it is a match, that is okay; you can reuse these steps to find another doctor option.

- ◊ Most primaries will require you to make a new patient appointment where they will do a general exam and review your medical history.
- ◊ You will want to try your hardest to find your perfect primary *before* you actually need a doctor for a medical issue.

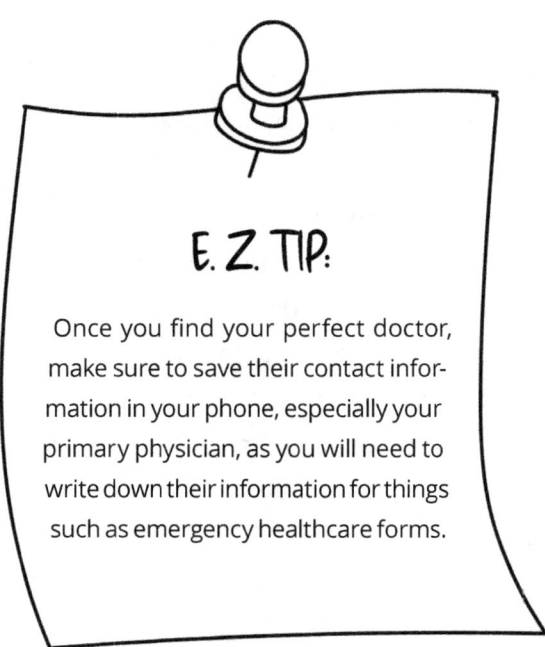

E. Z. TIP:

Once you find your perfect doctor, make sure to save their contact information in your phone, especially your primary physician, as you will need to write down their information for things such as emergency healthcare forms.

Also, make sure you know what urgent care and hospital options you prefer to go to in case of an emergency. Knowing where these places are beforehand can save precious time and stress. Add these options to your contact list as well so you don't have to scramble to find them during an emergency situation.

MEDICATION INSPIRATION

- Medication usage is something that people feel different about, whether it be strongly for or against medication usage.
- FORM YOUR OWN OPINION! It is YOUR body and YOUR choice! And do not ever forget that!!!
- Nobody knows your body as you do, not even a doctor. Remember, fancy degrees and certifications do not automatically mean that person will have your best interests in mind.
- On the flip side, there are more doctors out there who do want to help you; finding the right one for you is just another example of the importance of self-educating.
- If you feel something is off, it is your right to find a new doctor and get a second opinion, or even multiple doctors and multiple opinions. It is your body, your choice!
- Being able to describe what is going on within yourself in detail will help doctors be able to treat you to the best of their abilities and increase the likelihood of finding the best medication for your situation.
  - ◊ With that in mind: DO NOT lie to your doctors about something you are experiencing just because it may be embarrassing to talk about. They are doctors; it is their job to take your concerns into account when forming a proper treatment plan, and I am willing to bet that they have seen and heard worse.
  - ◊ Making a list of your symptoms, concerns, and questions *before* going to your appointment is a great way to keep your thoughts in order.
- Before taking a new medication, read about it first so you know what it is supposed to do and what negative side effects it could cause that you should look out for.

- Having medications filled and refilled is as simple as finding a pharmacy that accepts your medical coverage.
    ◊ Many noncontrolled substances can be filled and shipped to you through online pharmacies.
    ◊ To save money, ask your doctor if there is a generic version of the medication: same drug, slightly different name, MUCH cheaper!
- If you decide it is time to try medication therapy for mental health struggles, it is a good idea to independently research medications before going to a doctor. Find medications that you believe will best suit your wants and needs, and understand the adverse effects that can occur and the general pros and cons.
- ADVOCATE for yourself! Do not let a doctor push drugs on you that you are uncomfortable taking.

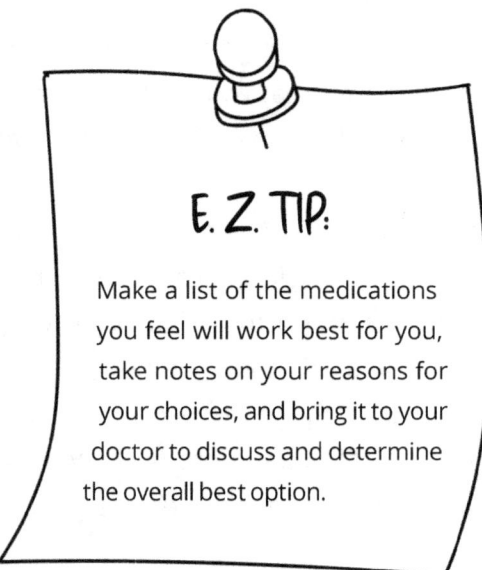

E. Z. TIP:

Make a list of the medications you feel will work best for you, take notes on your reasons for your choices, and bring it to your doctor to discuss and determine the overall best option.

SELF-CARE & PRESERVATION

Take this information into consideration to help prevent a sticky situation!

Unfortunately, we live in a world filled with dishonest people and crimes, ranging anywhere from violent to mental to the theft of your personal belongings. Being **proactive** to protect yourself from crimes is crucial.

> **Proactive**: Being proactive means exercising control over a situation in a manner that affects the outcome rather than waiting to react to a situation after it has already happened.
> - Installing security measures around your home, such as cameras and floodlights, before an act of theft occurs is an example of being proactive, whereas installing these safety measures after an incident occurs is reactive.

ROBBERY PREVENTION/PROTECTION

- Make sure ALL doors and windows are locked before leaving or going to bed.
- Make sure all exterior doors have a dead bolt.
  - ◊ A dead bolt lock can only be opened with a key or handle, whereas typical doorknob locks are equipped with a spring-bolt-type lock that can be easily opened when force is applied to it.

E. Z. DID IT TIP:

Porch pirates used to steal my packages all the time; nothing has been taken since my camera went up! However, before I could afford a real camera, I crafted a brightly colored sign that indicated I had a camera hidden out of sight. That kept my packages from being stolen as well.

- Do not forget to lock the door between your garage and the rest of your home.
  - ◊ Many people forget this door, and many criminals know it!
- Make it look like somebody is home, even when they're not.
  - ◊ Leave a couple of lights on and have a radio playing.
    - + Talk radio or a podcast would be great!
  - ◊ Close blinds so people can't see if you are at home or not.

Porch Pirates: This refers to people who steal packages from other people's homes.

- Do not display "flashy" or expensive items for people to see and want to take from you.
- Cameras! Have security cameras installed pointing at home entry points, such as exterior doors and first-floor windows. Also make sure to protect other areas on your property that people could break into, such as sheds and garages.
  - ◊ You can find cameras to fit your needs at all price points. If you can't afford a real one, buy a decoy — anything helps.

VEHICLE THEFT PREVENTION & PROTECTION

- LOCK YOUR DOORS! Many people these days check car doors, and if they're unlocked, your possessions become *fair* game.
- Remove or hide valuable items. Lock things in your trunk if possible.
- Roll your windows all the way up.
- Park in well-lit, nonsecluded areas.

VIOLENT CRIME PREVENTION & PROTECTION

- KNOW THE AREA! It is no secret that some places are more dangerous than others. Be familiar with places that you should not go to alone, after dark, etc.
- Try to avoid walking alone at night no matter where you are. Also, make sure you are *constantly* paying attention to your surroundings.
  - ◊ Phones down, eyes up, people!
- Keep pepper spray or something to protect yourself in your purse, bag, car, pocket, etc.

SELF-DEFENSE

This is a scary topic to think about, but knowing how to protect yourself and put up a fight if the situation arises is important. Here are some effective moves to think of and practice to protect yourself as much as possible:

Hammer hit: When walking alone, hold your car keys with the pointy ends sticking out of your fist, and use that to strike your attacker.

THE HAMMER CLAW!

THE GROIN KICK!

Groin kick: A hard knee or fist to the groin is always good!

Palm hit: Flex your wrist so your palm is out. Use the heel of your palm to strike the attacker. Aim for the nose, throat, or chin!

BAM!

Bear hug escape: If an attacker grabs you from behind, bend forward to shift your weight to your advantage, then throw your elbows back to jab the attacker, and when you have the room, turn and give a good groin kick, then RUN.

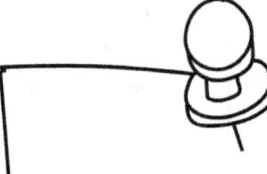

E. Z. TIP:

Trust your instincts. If something doesn't feel right, DO NOT DO IT! Claw, kick, push, spit, scream, mace, tase, punch... do what you have to do to protect yourself!!!

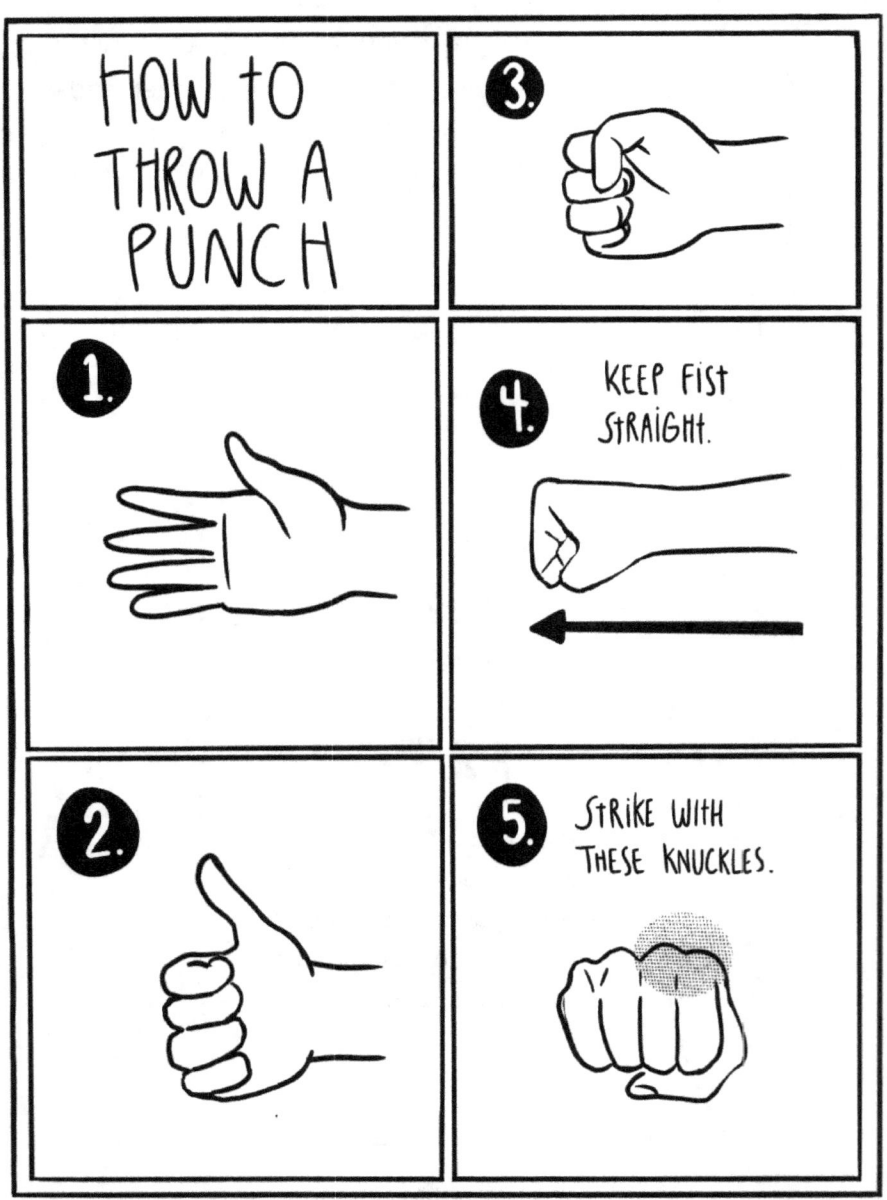

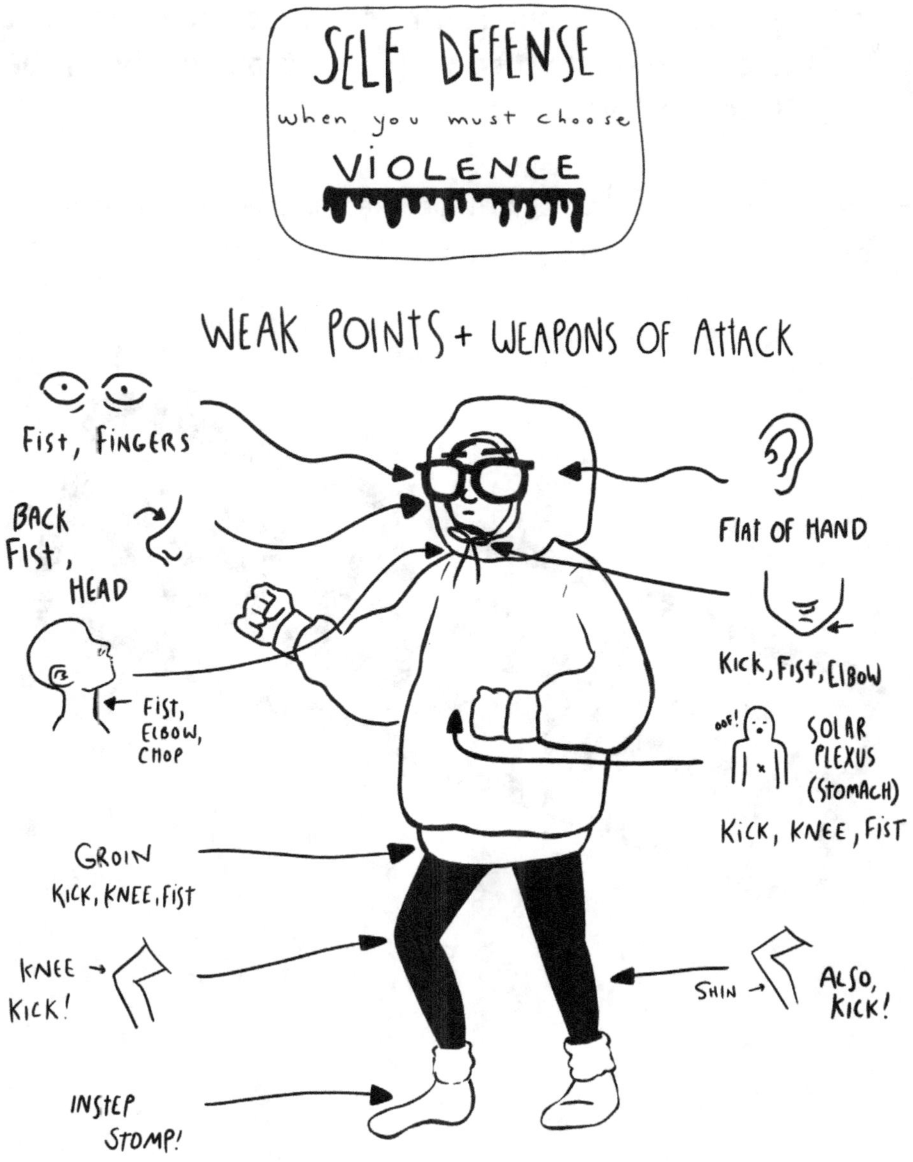

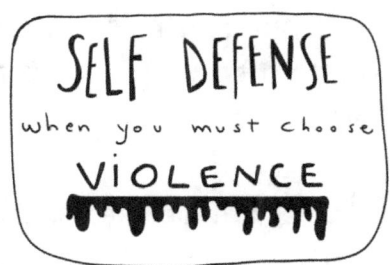

SELF DEFENSE
when you must choose
VIOLENCE
WEAK POINTS + WEAPONS OF ATTACK
FIST, FINGERS
BACK FIST, HEAD
FIST, ELBOW, CHOP
GROIN
KICK, KNEE, FIST
KNEE → KICK!
INSTEP STOMP!
FLAT OF HAND
KICK, FIST, ELBOW
OOF!
SOLAR PLEXUS (STOMACH)
KICK, KNEE, FIST
SHIN →
ALSO, KICK!

 # TREAT YO-SELF POP QUIZ!

Great news! This quiz has been canceled too. It seems mean to throw a pop quiz at the end of the Treat Yo-Self chapter!

However, I have included a mental health checkup exercise in **Appendix E**. Give it a scan if you'd like, or don't. Your book, your choice!

Use this space to start planning out your journey to adulting happiness!

_____

_____

_____

_____

_____

_____

_____

_____

_____

_____

_____

_____

_____

_____

_____

_____

_____

_____

_____

_____

_____

_____

_____

_____

_____

_____

_____

_____

_____

_____

_____

_____

_____

_____

_____

_____

_____

_____

_____

_____

_____

SO YOU GRADUATED HIGH SCHOOL. WHAT NOW?

?!

TIME TO START MAKING SOME BIG DECISIONS, BUT BIG DOES NOT HAVE TO MEAN SCARY!

 Keep reading to find a personal story/informational section combo platter! Gotta keep things interesting and expect the unexpected, just like life!

CONGRATS! YOU'RE A HIGH SCHOOL GRADUATE!

It's time to start putting all that education to good use!

I am going to mix it up here a bit and combine my chapter introduction story with my first informational section. This was not an easy choice as a person who thrives on a routine and structure. However, life can throw you curve-balls out of nowhere that will knock you off your routine. Think of this remix here as just that. Reset your frame of mind and just dive in headfirst!

Congratulations! Here is your diploma. Now tell us what you plan to do with your life. *Right. Now.*

Your *official* first step into the adulting world can be incredibly overwhelming; I can't even lie to you there. You just survived high school, and now you are expected to know who you are and what you want to do with your life. For society to think that any 18-year-old brain is equipped to handle such a complex, life-altering decision has always seemed like such a joke.

Sure, you may have an idea based on your passions and hobbies you've collected along the way to this point; but that does not dictate your life's path. It is *your* life, and you are in control of your thoughts and actions. At the end of the day, you have to live with those, so you better make them count!

Fun fact: I have been in love with animals for my entire life. No joke, just ask my folks! I am pretty sure I started telling people that I wanted to be a veterinarian when I was too young to even really know what a vet was. I sure as heck can tell you that you will never find a single school assignment or diary entry gushing about how much I loved the idea of teaching and that I saw my future in the education field!

Nope. Nada. Zip. And look at me now!

I couldn't imagine not doing what I am doing and teaching what I teach; I absolutely love what I do. My desire to see my students succeed in their lives is so strong that I wrote a book for them, for you, and for anybody else brave enough to soak in what I have to say.

Let me give you a semi-quick synopsis as to how I got from *there* to *here*. As soon as I was old enough, I was determined to find a job at an animal hospital. After putting in the work, I landed a job that I loved; the people were great, and learning as much about animals as possible was terrific. I couldn't get enough of it. As I spent more time in the industry, I realized that while I wanted to have a career with animals, I no longer felt that being a veterinarian was my true calling.

I will spare you the details on how I came to make that decision; all that matters is that I felt it was the best choice for my life. I still do.

Telling family and friends that I changed my mind on something I was very vocal about my entire life wasn't ideal, but I refuse to live my life for others, and I want to be happy with my choices. While that was a huge decision I made, I'm going to be honest: I had no idea what I wanted to do instead.

I still loved learning about animal welfare and medical care, so I decided to go to school to become a registered veterinary technician. I graduated with my veterinary technology degree, passed my board exams, and got a job in an animal shelter.

I hated it.

It did not take long to realize I could not mentally handle what I was going to be trained to do, and I was starting to wonder where my path would lead me. This was a scary realization to come to, but also a bit of an exciting one as well!

My path led me to visit my former high school veterinary assistant teacher, a woman whose love of animals always inspired me and somebody I looked up to as a role model. That visit turned into learning about, applying for, and accepting a position as the teacher assistant for that same program. Now here we are: over 10 years, 3.5 college degrees, and a teacher certification later, I am co-teaching alongside that person I visited that one fateful day.

One casual visit to complain about how I wasn't sure what to do with my life ended up changing my life. Everything is meant to happen the way it is supposed to.

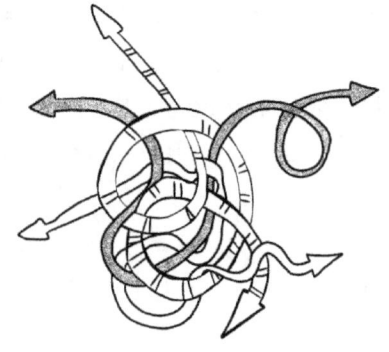

Getting to the point in my life that I am at now, the point where I felt like writing a "self-help" book on adulting was something I was qualified to do, was not pretty. Not pretty at all. I made mistakes, doubted myself, lost sleep, and cried to family and friends — the whole dramatic shebang.

It is messy, but it is my story, and I wouldn't change a thing. I began to seek out lessons in my past actions and consequences. I could step back and see the kind of person I wanted to be, which forced me to realize I had a lot of self-work to do, and I put a conscious effort into making those changes within myself every single day.

Ultimately, you are the only one capable of truly changing yourself. My apologies for the super-cheesy motivational line there, but it's a goody, and this seemed like a great place to slip it in. I feel the need to tell you that I could not type the end of that sentence without giggling to myself a bit. Adulting doesn't always have to be serious!

I still have work to do on myself, I still have tough days, and I definitely still have days when I am tempted to run back to my parents' home and hide in my old basement fort, but that is okay, and that is real, honest life. I have the hunger to continue learning as much about how the world works as I can, continually growing and evolving using what I have learned as my instrument of change. I am living my life the way I feel is best, and I will not apologize for it.

The moral of this "educational" story is that it is okay if you don't know what you want to do with every upcoming chapter in your life. I would be mildly concerned if any high school graduate had firmly mapped out the next 50 years of their life. Who you were in high school is not who you will be or have to be as an adult.

Shoot, who you were before and after reading this book could be different, and there is nothing wrong with that.

There is no set curriculum and schedule for personal growth. It is also okay if you change your mind regarding a decision you once were passionate about. Make the choices you feel are right, and don't be apologetic for putting *your* goals and dreams first.

So, you graduated high school. What now?

The answer to that is nobody's business but your own.

CONTINUING YOUR EDUCATION

Going to college is YOUR choice, and it should be an educated one!

So you decided to go the college route? That is great! This section aims to help you choose the best continuing education decision for you.

Whether you are planning to enroll in college right after you graduate or you make the choice to go back at any point in your adult life, it is a big, important step no matter what age you are. "Educating" yourself on how to start this journey will make it easier.

To give you a quick snapshot of my journey, I went to college right after graduation and then back several more times over the last 12 or so years. This is a topic I have a lot of experience in.

Here are the steps I like to go through when it comes to deciding what to take and where to take it. Rest assured, these steps are E. Z.-tested and -approved!

- First things first: What **type of degree** are you seeking?
  - ◊ Are you wanting these courses to advance in your career or get you started on your future career journey?
  - ◊ **Example:** I needed a degree in agriculture to qualify for my teaching position; the degree needed to be a bachelor's or above. I already had a bachelor's degree, and I knew graduate courses would place me at a better starting point on the teacher salary.

Types of Degrees: The following are types of degrees and, on average, how many credit hours are required to complete each degree.

- Associate's degree: Minimum of 60 credit hours
- Bachelor's degree: Minimum of 120 credit hours
- Master's degree: On average, 30–60 credit hours
- Doctoral degree: On average, 60–120 credit hours
  - ◊ Please note: College classes are measured by credit hours. The number of credit hours per course is equivalent to the average number of hours you will spend on that particular course per week.
    - + One credit typically represents one hour spent in class and two hours spent on homework.
    - + One three-credit course will equal approximately nine hours of work per week.

I am all about working smarter and not harder, so I decided to look for a master's degree in agriculture. After a TON of research, I found a master's degree in agricultural education that I could complete online — exactly what I wanted!

Believe me when I tell you that it took me hours of persistent googling to find that degree. Don't be afraid to dig deep and put in the research time, especially with a decision like this!

That example leads me to my next step. Once you have a solid idea of the type of degree you want and your chosen area of focus you would like to major in, it is time to start looking.

- The internet is a beautiful thing. Use it, and make sure you find a **credible degree at a credible institution** to save yourself from a whole lot of potential stress on your psyche and wallet!

Credible Degrees & Institutions: Attending an accredited college will ensure your hard work is going toward a degree that will be recognized by potential employers and other institutions you may want to transfer to in the future. Research the following information to help determine whether the college you are interested in is legitimate.

- Know that schools can be accredited at national, regional, or international levels. Most colleges in the United States will have an institutional accreditation they received from a regional agency.
- Go to the school's site and look for its accreditation status. Most institutions will provide a link to this information on their home page.
- BEFORE enrolling, make sure that both the college AND the degree you seek are truly accredited. Certain degrees may require specialized accreditation, and just because the college is accredited doesn't automatically mean all their degrees are.

- Check to see if the college you are interested in is accredited by the **US Department of Education (USDE)** or the **Council for Higher Education Accreditation (CHEA).**
    - ◊ If you pursue a nonaccredited, lesser-known college, you will likely not be able to receive federal and state financial aid. Also, your degree may not be recognized, and if you transfer to an accredited college, your credits will likely not be **eligible to transfer**. *Accreditation is important!*

US Department of Education: An agency of the federal government that establishes, coordinates, and enforces policy for most federal assistance to education. They help the president execute nationwide education policies and implement laws that are enacted by Congress.

Check out their site for more information.

ed.gov

Council for Higher Education Accreditation (CHEA): The only national organization in the US that focuses solely on higher education accreditation and quality assurance. The CHEA is governed by a board of 20 members that are made up of college/university presidents, public members, and institution representatives. They advocate for higher academic quality for accreditation on both national and international levels, as well as provide a communication platform for accredited institutions.

Check out their site for more information.

chea.org

Eligible to Transfer: The only surefire way to determine whether your credits will be transferable to a new college is by contacting the institution and asking about it. You will want to ensure you have all your course information handy: college details, course names/codes, and credit hour information. Your transcripts should have all of this information.

Here are some things to think about when it comes to transferring credits:

- Take courses through well-known, established institutions. There are a ton of tiny colleges out there. Some colleges may not accept transfer credits from lesser-known institutions.
- Obtain a course catalog from the college you are interested in transferring to. This will give you an idea of what credits will transfer and what you will need to take to complete your education goal.
  - ◊ This should be easily accessible on the college website.
- Many colleges have a specific cap on the number of credits they will allow new students to transfer over; the type of degree you seek may also impact that number.
- Validate your credit transferability BEFORE officially enrolling in a new institution. If you are unhappy with their offer, you can attempt to appeal their decision or find a college that better fits your needs.
- If you are changing majors or seeking a bachelor's degree after obtaining your associate's degree, keep in mind that a lot of your courses may transfer over and only fill up the number of elective credits required for that degree. You will likely still have to take many courses to satisfy your new degree requirements.

- Double- (and triple-) check that you meet the qualifications needed to be considered for the program you are interested in, as well as what you need to do to apply.
  - ◊ I've applied for colleges requiring different combinations of letters of recommendation, personal statements, writing samples, high school/college transcripts, and application submission fees.
    - + Yes, many colleges require a payment just to apply! *Madness!*
  - ◊ Applying to colleges can be a long, tedious process. I recommend applying only to colleges you are seriously interested in. I also recommend finding a couple of options that you like.
    - + Having a fallback plan is always an excellent idea for when life happens! Which is often!
  - ◊ Here's an E. Z. tried-and-true tip to help you keep the above information nice and organized: Make a chart or take notes on the different colleges and degree programs you are most interested in so you can easily compare and settle on the best option(s) for you.
- Once you have a solid idea of your top choice(s), set up a meeting to tour the campus, unless you are seeking an online degree. Speak to an **academic advisor** and communicate with their financial aid department to ensure you will be able to pay for tuition.

Academic Advisor: The role of an academic advisor is to act as a mentor of sorts when it comes to helping you understand and realize college and career options that are best suited for your goals.

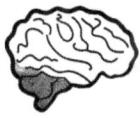

FINANCIAL AID *FUN*

So, you made an educated decision as to where you want to enroll. What now? Now comes the fun part, the money part...

By this point, you should have at least some loosely formed plans regarding the route you need to take to fund your education. Make sure the schools you are looking into accept the type of payment that you need to use at a tuition cost you are comfortable with.

There are all sorts of ways to fund a college education; you just have to look for them. Again, another critical facet of adulting that requires deep research to yield the best results. The powers that be do not often make it easy to get free money!

Don't fret; the types of funding are broken down later in this section.

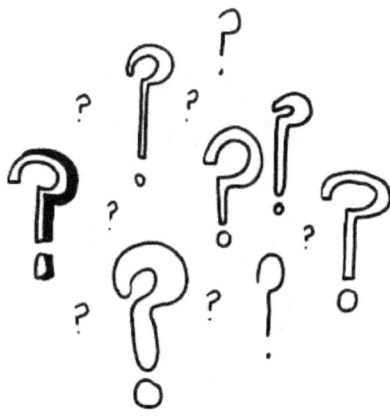

- Check out all the incentives offered by the colleges you are interested in, such as tuition breaks for those interested in work-study programs.
  - ◊ For example, I attended a university that gave me a 50% tuition break for being a public school teacher in the area.
- It is always worth checking out the colleges in your state. Many colleges offer tuition breaks for in-state students. Some colleges may extend that offer to students from neighboring states as well.
- Note that some schools that accept financial aid may not accept it for all the programs they offer.
  - ◊ I enrolled in a college for a certificate program only to find out that the university did not take financial aid for certificates for some reason. Had I found that out earlier, it would have saved me a lot of time and disappointment... oh, and the money wasted on the application fee!

FAFSA *FUN*

If you are unable to pay for college on your own and will need some type of financial aid, you are going to want to fill out the Free Application for Federal Student Aid (FAFSA).

If you *are* able to pay for your tuition with no help, it is still a good idea to fill out the FAFSA to cover yourself in case funding falls through. Make sure you pay attention here.

WHAT IS THE FAFSA, YOU ASK?

- It is a form prospective, current, or returning students needing aid must fill out before enrolling in college.
- It collects personal and financial data of the student, then uses that information to determine what aid, if any, you qualify for.
    - ◊ Please note, if you still live with a parent or guardian, you may have to include their financial information as well, whether or not they are helping you with tuition.
- VERY IMPORTANT! You want to ensure you fill out and submit your FAFSA as quickly as possible once it opens. Especially if you think you will qualify for any type of grants or scholarships.
    - ◊ Please note, FAFSA opening and submission dates have changed a few times since the pandemic.
    - ◊ State deadlines for FAFSA submissions can vary as well.
    - ◊ Head over to the U.S. Department of Education site to locate specific state requirements.
        - + ed.gov/about/contacts/state/index.html
- It determines the exact type of aid you qualify for: grants, work-study opportunities, scholarships, different loan types, etc.
- IMPORTANT! Grants, scholarships, and other types of financial assistance are often distributed on a first-come, first-served basis. Get your application submitted as quickly as possible if you believe you qualify for extra assistance.
    - ◊ If you don't know exactly what school you want to attend by October 1, you can submit your FAFSA with several school options you are interested in applying for.

◊ You can also go back into your FAFSA account to change and resubmit any information as needed.

WHAT DO YOU NEED TO KNOW BEFORE YOU FILL OUT THE FAFSA?

- EVERYTHING!
- It is imperative that you fully understand the FAFSA and its importance before submitting one.
- Head over to the FAFSA site to get all your questions answered appropriately.
    - ◊ studentaid.gov
    - ◊ Make sure you do your research on the official government-derived site (.gov) to ensure you do not get scammed!

COMMON FINANCIAL AID TYPES:

- **Loans:** College financial aid loans are just like any other type of loan. It is money that you are borrowing and will be required to pay back.
    - ◊ There are multiple student loan options you can take out, depending on your situation.
    - ◊ Pay close attention to repayment and interest rates when deciding what kind of loan to take out.
- **Scholarships:** This is free money given to students by various organizations. Typically, a student must fit within a list of requirements to be eligible for the scholarship. There is a TON of different types of scholarships available to different types of people and situations. Put in the work to find and apply for scholarships you are eligible for, and it could result in FREE money for your schooling!

- **Grants:** This is another option for a student to receive financial aid that is not required to be paid back. Different types of federal grants are available to people who fall within certain parameters. If you think you may qualify for grant money, it is very important that you submit your FAFSA as close to the October 1st opening date as possible.
    - ◊ Keep in mind, some grants and scholarships may come with rules the student is required to follow to receive the entire financial aid package being offered. Breaking the agreement could result in loss of the aid and having to repay the money you received. Read the fine print!
- **Work-study:** Some schools offer work-study opportunities to students, which involve the student working part-time and earning money to go toward education costs. Work-study programs will differ from school to school, so make sure you look into options for the specific institute you plan to attend.

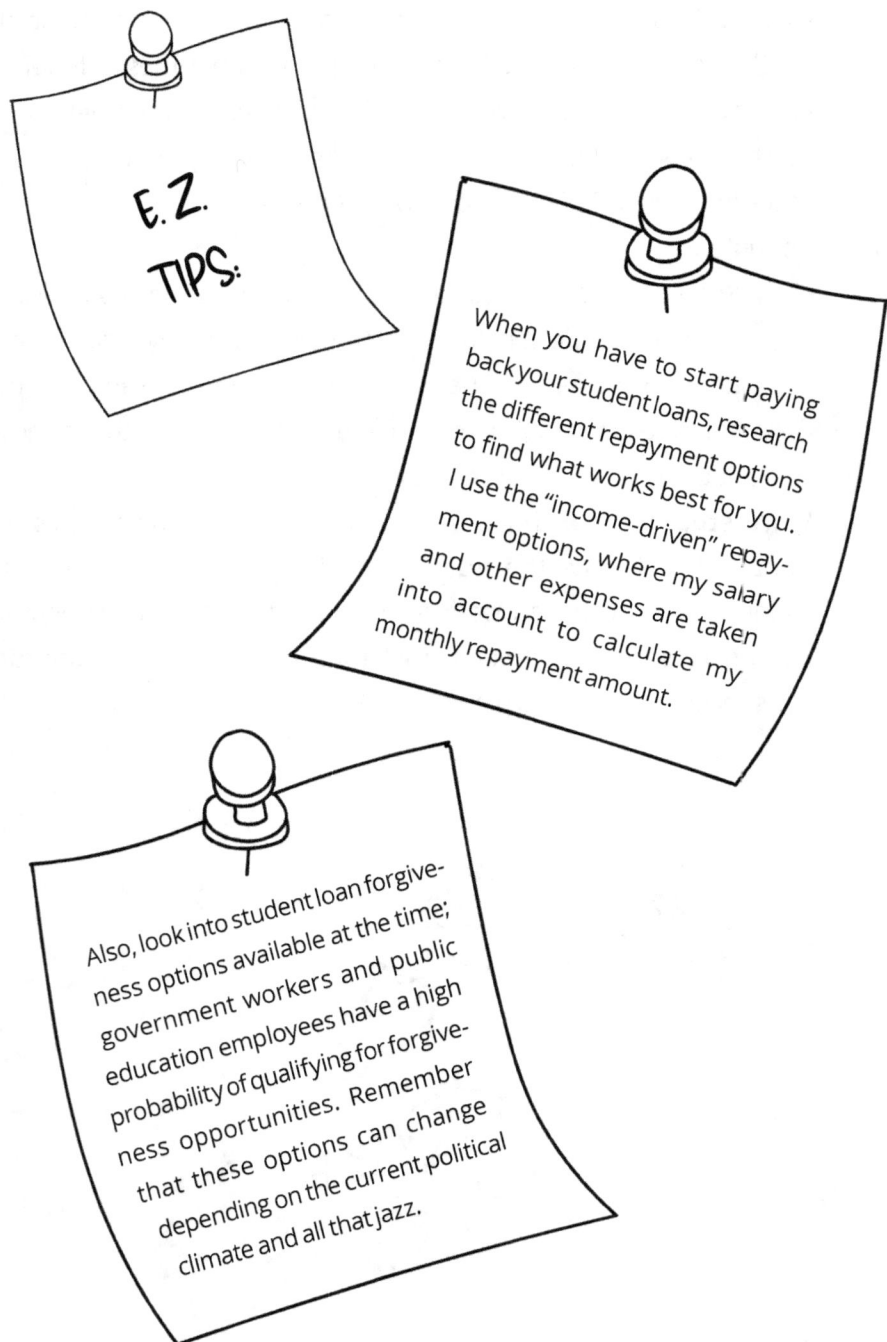

E. Z.
TIPS:

When you have to start paying back your student loans, research the different repayment options to find what works best for you. I use the "income-driven" repayment options, where my salary and other expenses are taken into account to calculate my monthly repayment amount.

Also, look into student loan forgiveness options available at the time; government workers and public education employees have a high probability of qualifying for forgiveness opportunities. Remember that these options can change depending on the current political climate and all that jazz.

TRANSFERRING COLLEGE CREDITS

Keep in mind that transferring to different colleges is not unheard of, and there is nothing wrong with changing your mind or your major. It is quite common for students to attend community colleges after graduating high school to knock out their general education courses at significantly lower tuition costs, then transfer to four-year universities to focus on their majors.

The following are tips and thoughts I talk to my students about every year:

- First, I recommend checking to see what scholarship programs are available in your state that you can secure while still in high school.
  - ◊ An example is the A+ program in Missouri. High school students must complete a specific number of tutoring hours to complete the program. Upon completion, the A+ program will pay for all or part of the students' tuition.

◊ Make sure you fully understand the requirements to complete this program properly and that you also understand the stipulations regarding what type of colleges accept this program's benefits.

+ This specific program will pay a student's tuition at any Missouri public community college, technical school, or vocational school. However, students must be enrolled full-time, and the program will only pay a maximum of $189 per credit hour.

+ **Please note:** This information could be subject to change.

◊ If you do not plan to go to any of the college options listed above, that doesn't necessarily mean you are totally out of luck. Contact the specific school you are interested in and ask if they offer any type of A+ program scholarship. It likely will not cover all of your tuition costs, but any amount of funding helps!

• Attending a public community college to complete your general studies is a great idea and a HUGE money saver. Though if you plan to transfer to a four-year university, you need to do some research regarding the transferring of credits from one institution to another, so you don't end up wasting precious time and money.

READY TO HIT THE WORKFORCE RUNNING

Put your best foot forward and start sprinting toward the job of your dreams!

Time to get a job! Whether you decide to continue your education or go straight into the workforce after graduation, it is essential to always maintain a certain level of professionalism to secure the job role you want.

Regardless of the profession you hope to get into, the steps I have provided below to help you apply and interview for a new job are essentially the same.

- First things first, create an up-to-date résumé that is ready to send out to different employment positions you are interested in.
  - ◊ Having a professional, well-done résumé is extremely important, as it will be the first impression you are making to your potential new employer.
  - ◊ A ton of free résumé-building templates are available on the internet. Find one that best fits the way you want to introduce yourself and your skills.
  - ◊ The following are details you will want or need to include in your professional résumé to be considered for the job you're applying to:
    - + NO spelling or grammar issues!

+ Information that shows employers the type of person you are, what makes you unique, and why you are the best fit for the job. Make sure your information is presented professionally and in a manner that comes off as **confident, NOT cocky**!

◊ Correct, up-to-date contact information, work and education history, certifications, awards, professional organization memberships, achievements, etc.

◊ A **professional** email address.

Confident vs. Cocky: A fine line runs between being confident and cocky. A confident person believes in themselves and their abilities, know their strengths and limitations, are humble, and are mindful, whereas a cocky person comes off as overly confident in a brash manner that annoys or frustrates others. Someone who comes off as cocky is more likely to be viewed as insecure and fake. Strive for confidence, not cockiness.

Professional: A professional email address will help you be taken more seriously in the professional world, plain and simple. Think of it as the way you virtually introduce yourself and make a first impression.

- The most common professional email format for young adults is FirstName.LastName@Domain.com.
- You can also simplify it down to your first name and last name initial or vice versa.

◊ References: make sure you get permission from references you want to include on your résumé beforehand. Most importantly, make sure the people you list as references will give you a positive, glowing recommendation!

◊ Skills you possess should pertain to the position you are applying for. If you need ideas on ways to best word your capabilities, simply use the search engine of your choice to help you out.

+ Search "(insert career here) job skill examples."

+ Make sure the skills you include on your résumé are clear-cut and straightforward, relevant to the position, a variety of both hard and soft skills, and ones that can set you apart from other applicants. Oh yeah, and make sure the skills you include on your résumé are ones that you actually have and feel confident performing!

Soft skills: Soft skills pertain to your personality and the traits you possess that make you the best candidate for the job.
- Examples include things such as good communication, leader-ship, flexibility, problem-solving, time management, empathy, optimism, etc.

Hard skills: These are technical skills you possess that you have acquired through education, training, and experience. You must include hard skills on your résumé that specifically relate to the job you are applying for.
- Examples include specific degrees and certifications you've earned, accounting, computer skills, spe-cific programs you know how to operate, etc.

- A **cover letter** introduces yourself and allows you to tell potential employers exactly why you are the best candidate for the job.
  - ◊ Not all job positions will require a cover letter to accompany your résumé when applying, but it will help set you apart from other applicants and aid you in making the best first impression possible.
  - ◊ A ton of cover letter templates and examples are available online to help you make sure you put together a letter that best represents the awesome person you are.

Cover Letter: This is a letter that you send in along with your résumé; this letter provides you with the opportunity to introduce yourself to potential employers better, explain why you want to work at their organization, and list reasons why you are the most qualified candidate for the job.

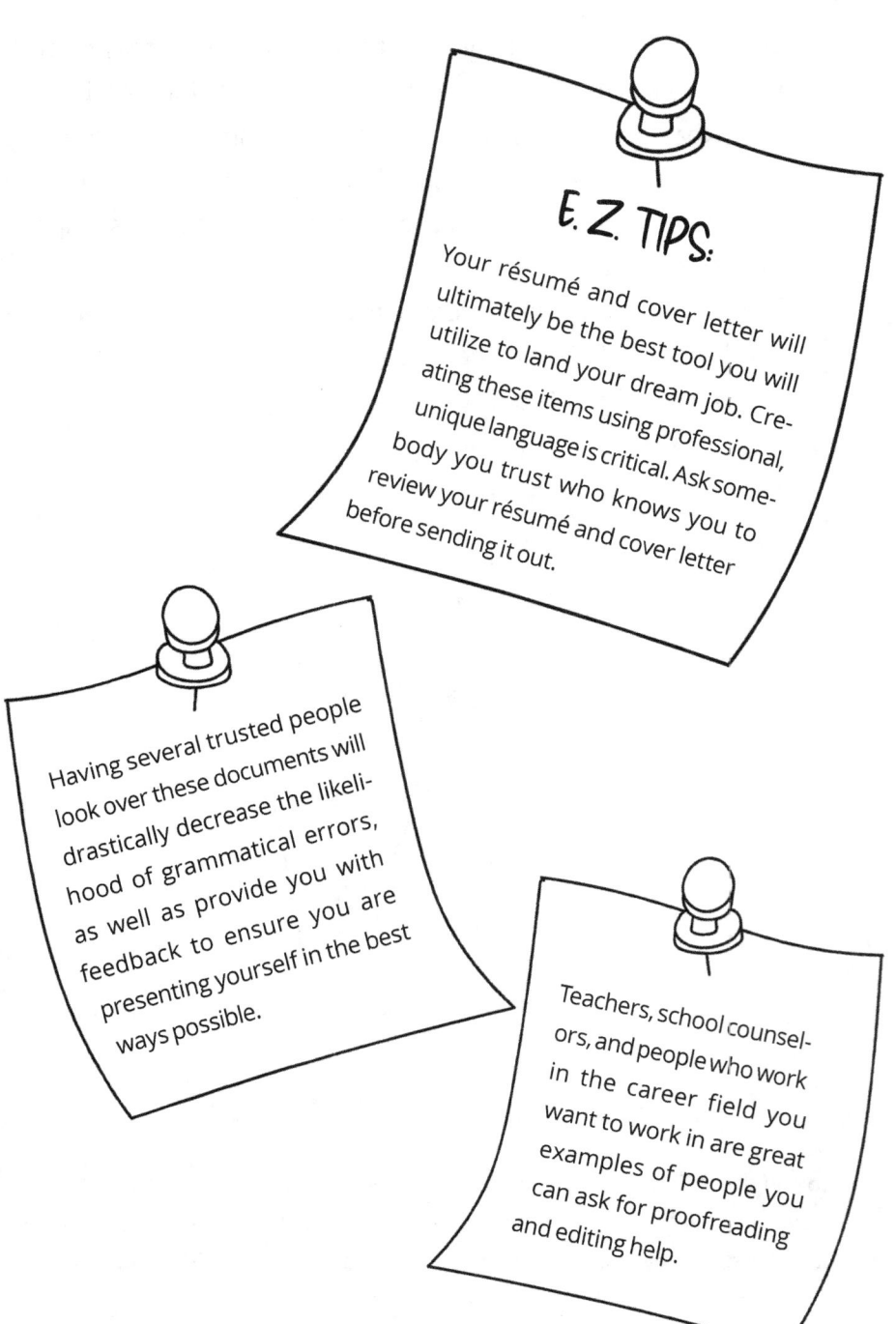

E. Z. TIPS:

Your résumé and cover letter will ultimately be the best tool you will utilize to land your dream job. Creating these items using professional, unique language is critical. Ask somebody you trust who knows you to review your résumé and cover letter before sending it out.

Having several trusted people look over these documents will drastically decrease the likelihood of grammatical errors, as well as provide you with feedback to ensure you are presenting yourself in the best ways possible.

Teachers, school counselors, and people who work in the career field you want to work in are great examples of people you can ask for proofreading and editing help.

- Find an employment position you are interested in. Make sure you read the job requirements and fit the needs they are looking for before applying; otherwise, you are just wasting your time. *READ THE FINE PRINT!*
- When you find a job opportunity that you are qualified for, the next step is to figure out how to apply for the position properly.
- Some companies may have an application you will need to complete and submit on their website, and others may just ask for a résumé to be emailed to a specific person.
  - ◊ If you don't apply correctly, you will likely not be considered for the position at all, no matter how perfect of a fit you may be. The application process will give a potential employer an idea of how well you follow directions.

E. Z. TIP:

Employers tend to really like people who can follow directions!

Refer to **Appendix F** for examples of both a good and bad résumé.

EXERCISE YOUR RIGHT TO VOTE!

Don't break a sweat when it comes to exercising your rights!
You earned them!

When you turn 18, you begin to unlock new levels of adulthood. One fundamental right you get to exercise once you are 18 is the right to vote! The following are tips to help you register to vote.

> Please keep in mind that registration rules, guidelines, and deadlines can differ depending on the state you live in.

- First, you MUST be a naturally born or full naturalized citizen of the United States to be able to vote.
- The easiest way to learn how to register to vote in your state is by visiting a website such as rockthevote.org or vote.gov.
  - ◊ From either site, you can pick your state of residence and get the specific information you need to register correctly and on time. Policies can vary from state to state.
- Make sure you have all the necessary information and meet all the requirements for both registering to vote and voting at the polls. Here are some things you will likely need:
  - ◊ The permanent address of your residence
  - ◊ Some type of identification
    - + **Photo ID examples**: driver's license, state ID card, military ID, passport, etc.
    - + **Nonphoto ID examples:** birth certificate, bank statement, Social Security card, utility bill, etc.

- As of 2021, a total of 42 states offer an online registration option to help the process be as seamless as possible for the new voter.
- The traditional mail and in-person registration processes are still an option in all states. Registration information can be mailed in or dropped off at your local election office.

 **YAY! You are officially a registered voter! Now what?** Well, now you get to exercise your right as a US citizen to vote for what you believe in. Here are some things to think about before hitting the polls.

- YOUR VOTE ABSOLUTELY MATTERS!
- Don't think about voting with an "I am only one person, with one vote, so it doesn't matter" mentality. If you and thousands or even millions of others have that same thought, then that can most definitely impact election results!
- Bring a valid ID with you to the polls, and make sure your state doesn't require anything else you need to show before voting.
- There are different ways to cast your ballot when election time rolls around.
    ◊ Again, please note the voting process can be different from state to state, so make sure you are looking at the specific information provided by the state of your permanent address.

- Voting options typically include:
    ◊ Voting in person at the polls
    ◊ Voting early
    ◊ Absentee voting

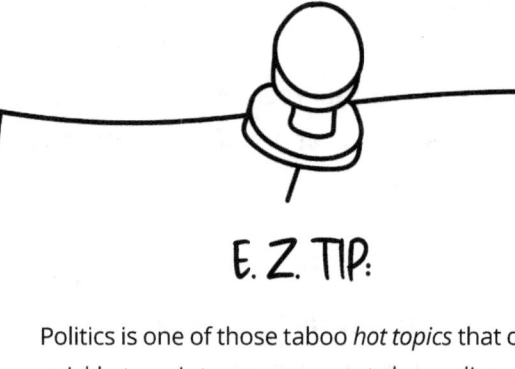

E. Z. TIP:

Politics is one of those taboo *hot topics* that can quickly turn into an argument depending on who you talk to and your personal political point of view. Regardless of this, I always encourage having open, healthy political conversations with people you know, those who have both the same and drastically different beliefs from you. Engage with people you feel comfortable with who you can ask open, honest questions and who can share their point of view without smothering you with it or belittling you.

I have learned a lot through having healthy conversations regarding touchy subjects with people. If I've said it once, I've said it a million times: I firmly believe that education is the key to eradicate ignorance. You will have a much harder time educating yourself on a topic if everyone avoids it. I promise you, it is possible to have mature conversations with people who do not share the same point of view with you, so don't be afraid to be open to the idea.

UNLOCKING LEVELS OF ADULTHOOD

It's like a real-life video game... with real-life consequences!

When you turn 18, you are considered an adult in many aspects of life. Before you get too crazy, it is important that you understand there are still things you cannot legally do for a few more years.

As you age, you will begin unlocking different rights and responsibilities, which you should be aware of. Here is a breakdown of adulting privileges that will open up to you once you reach a certain age:

- **18 years old:**
    - ◊ You are legally considered an adult. Yippy!
    - ◊ You can move out of your parents'/guardians' home.
    - ◊ You can be tried as an adult in a court of law.
    - ◊ You can be selected for jury duty and serve as a juror.
    - ◊ You can change your birth name.
    - ◊ You can get tattoos and piercings.
    - ◊ You can vote!
    - ◊ You can get a job that involves serving alcohol.
    - ◊ You can get credit cards and banking accounts on your own.
    - ◊ You can join the military.
    - ◊ You can file a lawsuit.
    - ◊ You can play the lottery.
    - ◊ You can apply for loans.
    - ◊ You can donate blood and become an organ donor.
    - ◊ You can purchase tobacco products.

◊ You can buy spray paint, superglue, fireworks, and other items that are deemed unsafe for minors to purchase.

- **21 years old:**
  - ◊ You are considered a "full-grown" adult, and you can get your adult license.
  - ◊ You can travel and book hotel rooms.
  - ◊ You can legally adopt a child.
  - ◊ You can legally purchase and consume alcoholic beverages.
  - ◊ You can go to bars, casinos, nightclubs, etc.
  - ◊ You can purchase recreational or medicinal cannabis in states where it has been legalized.
  - ◊ You can apply to carry and conceal.
- **25 years old:**
  - ◊ You can legally rent a vehicle.
- **35 years old:**
  - ◊ You can legally be in the running for being the next president of the United States. (You also must be a natural-born US citizen who has resided in the US for 14 years.)

Please note: These rights and responsibilities may unlock at different ages, depending on the state (or country) you call home.

 # SO YOU GRADUATED HIGH SCHOOL. WHAT NOW? POP QUIZ!

Who doesn't love a pop quiz? Especially one where there are no wrong answers?!

Read each question and really take the time to ponder the answers — not how you *THINK* you should answer, but how you *WANT* to answer! Use the blank space below to write down your answers or anything you'd like. It is your book, after all!

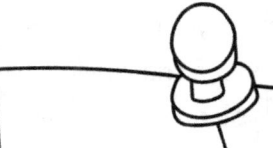

E. Z. TIP:

To make this book personal to your life, write down your answers in the area provided and leave yourself some space to revamp your responses as you experience the different twists and turns of your adulting journey.

QUIZ QUESTIONS

The following are common questions you may be asked during an interview with a potential employer. Carefully ponder these questions, formulate answers that will best highlight your skills, and be ready to dazzle the room!

1. Tell us about yourself.
2. What career goals do you have?
3. What is your past work history like?
4. Why did you leave your last position (or why do you want to leave)?
5. Why do you want to work here? How did you hear about this position?
6. Where do you see yourself in the future if you were to get this position?

7. What are your strengths?

8. What are your weaknesses? WORST question ever... but a popular one! I recommend doing some internet research to learn how to answer this question for yourself most appropriately! (Head back to the "How to Properly Utilize the Internet to Research" section at the beginning of your book for some refresher tips if needed.)

9. Tell us about a challenging experience within your professional life. How did you deal with this?

10. How would you describe your ideal work environment?

11. What are some of the professional achievements that you are most proud of? Why?

12. What are your salary and benefits expectations? (This is your chance to advocate for yourself and what you deserve!)

13. What type of leadership practices do you most value? Or what type of leadership practices do you plan to implement if you were to be in a managerial role?

14. What skill sets do you possess that make you unique and best qualified to fill this role?

15. Do you have any questions for us?

E. Z. TIP:

You want to have a few questions prepared and ready to ask. This will show potential employers that you are serious about the position you are interviewing for!

Use this space to start planning out your journey
to adulting happiness!

_____

_____

_____

_____

_____

_____

_____

_____

_____

_____

_____

_____

_____

_____

_____

_____

_____

E. Z. & FRIENDS' TIPS FOR SMART ADULTING

LIVE YOUR LIFE HOW YOU'D LIKE,
BUT ALWAYS BE OPEN TO LEARNING FROM OTHERS.

You made it! Welcome to the last chapter and the last story detailing all the weird and magical things I have experienced thus far in my adulting journey. I saved one of my favorite tales for this section, so buckle up! The moral of this story is that it is easier and more satisfying to be kind to others than to be rude.

E. Z. DID IT!

In my younger adult years, I could be very pushy regarding conversation topics or life experiences that I felt passionate about. I would argue until I was blue in the face to try and get my point across and show that I was *right*. This often involved inserting my opinions wherever I saw fit, even if they were unwanted. Not my most shining personality trait, I can admit now. It is a part of my journey, and I will own up to it. I feel like it is a phase many people go through in their young adult lives; maybe even you will.

As I grow both mentally and emotionally, I have learned to understand that what is *right* for me isn't automatically right for others. Who was I to tell a person what to do? At what point did I think I knew all the answers? It is fair to say I did *not* know all the answers, but I was getting really good at alienating people I loved with my blunt opinions and overall stubbornness.

As I type these words, I can proudly say that I have reached a place in my life where I value happiness and contentment, in whatever form that takes, and I want that feeling for everyone.

If it truly makes a person happy, then who am I to judge them? I don't care who a person loves, worships, respects, whatever; as long as it is not hurting anyone else or is illegal, *do you,* I say!

I reckon years and years of being surrounded by teenagers and animals taught me patience, resiliency, and how to lighten the hell up so I wouldn't go crazy! This is a mindset I am grateful for and one I will work hard to keep maintained and healthily cultivated for the rest of my days.

Okay, enough enlightened rambling; it's story time!

Over the years, it is becoming more common and accepted for people to feel safe enough to identify with their true selves, whether that be their chosen sexual orientations, gender identities, religious preferences, or any other trait that makes a person diverse (and happy).

With that in mind, I do my best to make it clear that my classroom is a safe place where people can express themselves how they want to, as long as that expression fits within the code of conduct for my school and classroom, of course. I have had the pleasure of teaching many students who identi-fied with various descriptions that fall on the LGBTQIA+ rainbow of love. I go out of my way to let students know that I will call them whatever they are comfortable with, whether it be a name that is not on the official roster or a gender pronoun they feel they most associate with. If it makes them feel happy and heard, it is my honor to respect their wishes.

I must admit, though, that it has not always been easy to remember the name and pronoun changes at all times. I have certainly slipped up and said the wrong things more than a few times, but I always make a conscious effort to be respectful and kind to others. Thankfully, my blunders have always been met with gracious understanding and positive encouragement.

One identifying pronoun has posed the greatest challenge for me, which I still struggle with to this day: the "they/them" pronoun. My reasons for this are purely grammatical. It has proven tough for me to use a plural pronoun for a singular person. It has been something that bothers me a bit, as I don't want to come off as being disrespectful or judgmental and hurt anyone's feelings.

We are getting to the point... I promise! A story such as this requires ample buildup!

Before I get too ahead of myself, this is probably a good time to mention I have a large variety of class pets in my program, including a baby tarantula that I added to the crew a couple of years ago. Fun fact about tarantulas: it is very difficult to determine their sexes as babies, as they typically do not reveal their genders until they are full-grown and have gone through several exoskeleton molts.

With that trivia fact in mind, I decided to name our new class pet Pat. I put a sign reading, *"Hi, my name is Pat, and I prefer they/them pronouns"* on their enclosure. When I introduced Pat to my students, I told everyone that I was using *them* as a teaching tool for *myself:* to teach my brain to use they/them pronouns in regards to a singular entity. I also explained that Pat could be a teaching tool for anybody else who needed the practice as I did.

I am going to be very honest here; I was *extremely* nervous at first to introduce Pat and the lesson they could teach to my students. Would they see a teacher trying to learn and be the best person she could be? Or would they be offended that I chose a giant, fluffy spider to practice they/them pronouns on?

For the record, I find tarantulas to be beautiful creatures! I call them spider puppies!

Sooooo... Pat turned out to be a spider that preferred to burrow and hide. They were not the most exciting, but it didn't stop me from regularly discussing Pat and how they chose to live their underground life. I always enjoyed sharing the lavish life tales of Pat. As long as I am a teacher, I hope to always have a "Pat" in my classroom.

I was relieved to learn that my students appreciated my efforts, seeing that I was taking this opportunity for self-growth and making it an option for everyone who met Pat. Even those who are terrified of spiders have been able to see Pat for what they represent and appreciate the lessons they bring!

Pat is an ambassador for positive changes and being kind to others!

WHAT'S IN IT FOR YOU!

It doesn't take extravagant measures to be a better version of yourself. While I can't always relate to the lifestyle choices I see people make, what I *can* see is that they appear happy and that their choices aren't hurting anyone or being destructive in any way. I wish everyone had that viewpoint, and I hope that I inspire others to think this way through my actions and words.

Words can tear down, and words can build up. When you spread enough hate, it starts to consume you, draining your energy and leaving you to feel empty inside at the end of the day. I hope you finish this book and are inspired to be the best version of yourself you can be! You can do it!

REAL ADULTING TIPS FROM REAL GROWN-UPS

Real-world advice from those who have really lived it.

The following *pearls of wisdom* have been shared with me by many wonderful grown-ups, all of whom want you to flourish into the Adulting World as much as me. Enjoy!

- Exercising self-control might just be the *HARDEST* part of adulting, but you need to do it to survive.
- You are about to enter the adult world, which means *YOU* are going to be 110% responsible for your actions. And that means *YOU* are also ´10% responsible for the consequences of those actions.
- Mommy and Daddy can no longer help you get out of things like they once could. Learn to stick up for yourself! Self-advocate!
- Read the fine print! Yes, it takes time to read it, but that is going to be where whomever you are dealing with is going to put all the most important details: penalty fees, horrific side effects, ownership of your soul, etc.

- Invest in the people who invest in you.
- Life is full of low lows and high highs. Learn how to approach these situations in a healthy manner and know you are not alone.
- You will never like everyone you meet in life, but you never know when you may run into them again and if you may need their help, so always be kind and keep it professional. *DON'T BURN BRIDGES!!!*
- Follow your gut! Listen to your instincts. If something seems too good to be true or off in any way, DON'T DO IT. *Trust your feelings!*
- You can't change people, only yourself.
- Whenever you attempt to repair anything, whether physical or emotional, keep this in mind: The last thing worked on should be the first thing checked.
- Remember the feeling of this time in your life, the confidence you have from knowing everything there is to know. As your life goes on, you'll still get that feeling, but it will likely come as a memory.
- If you do not know the answer to something, rather than immediately ask someone else for help, try and find the answer on your own. Self-educate!
- Know where to look for reputable information sources. Research your topic from all angles to best understand it and then make an educated decision on how to proceed. The more you do this, the more you will learn, the more you will likely retain that information, and the more self-sufficient you will become.

- MEMORIZE YOUR SOCIAL SECURITY NUMBER! You will need to use your Social Security number, or the last four digits, for essential purposes such as tax forms, work information, opening a new bank/credit account, etc. Having it written down and carrying it around with you can increase your chances of having your identity stolen or being scammed. They can't steal a memory!
- Lists! Adulting gets hectic sometimes, and you may feel like you are being pulled in many directions. If you've gotten this far in the book, you know that forgetting tasks can lead to costly or negative consequences. A crucial part of effective adulting is figuring out a way to remember things. A list is a great way to do this.
  - ◊ Make different lists for different task types, such as household maintenance needs, classwork, job tasks, and social reminders, such as loved ones' birthdays, anniversaries, etc.
  - ◊ Use a calendar to write reminders on, to break tasks down better, and help you prioritize what needs to be done first.
- When going to parties, *NEVER* leave open containers unattended and *NEVER* accept drinks from someone you do not know. Always stay with the people you arrived with, and of course, do NOT drink if you are underage.
- When buying food, toiletries, and other necessities, pass up the name brands and buy generic ones. You will save a lot of money!
  - ◊ Many products are made the exact same way, in the exact same place, just packaged differently and priced based on the package.

- Before you buy something that is not a need, hold it in front of you and ask yourself if you will still like it in a year? If you answer no, don't waste the money.
- If you miss too many days of classes and fail, you still have to pay tuition, so do your best not to miss class unless you absolutely have to. Find the study habits that work best for you and stick with them.
- Life is short. If you are in a situation where you are unhappy, whether it be personal or professional, *FIX IT*. You only get this one life!

I'm going to end this section with my special spin on a bit of a cliché quote, but it's a goody:

You will miss 100% of the shots you do not take. Don't be afraid to take chances, especially if there is the potential for bettering yourself!

SOCIAL(IZATION) MEDIA TIPS

What you put out there on the internet cannot always be erased.

Social media makes it easy for people to connect, whether the connection is positive or negative. The following are some things to consider regarding using these tools appropriately.

- First things first, clean up your social media!!!
  - ◊ *NOW* is the time to go through your social media accounts and delete or hide inappropriate photos, comments, posts, partying pictures, pictures showing too much skin, PDA relationship pictures, etc.
  - ◊ These posts can cost you a potential job, as many employers search social media accounts and will judge you by what they see before deciding if they want to meet you in real life to determine if you are a good candidate for that job position.
  - ◊ You can lock down your different social media accounts, making it impossible for strangers to view your information.

Remember that there could still be a way to get around your privacy protections. *Practice safe socials!*

◊ THINK BEFORE YOU POST!

- Make sure you have an email account with a professional name to use for business purposes.
  - ◊ Professionals will have difficulty communicating business with a peer whose email address is something like 2Hawt2Handle@ immaturity.com!
- *BE CAREFUL WHAT YOU POST!* Posting about being out of town is basically advertising that your home is empty and increases burglary chances. Post AFTER the trip.
- It takes a lot of time and hard work to build up a positive reputation and be respected; it takes very little time to lose that standing.
  - ◊ If this happens, pick yourself up, learn a lesson, and then put in the work to build yourself up better than before.
  - ◊ Reacting negatively is only going to dig yourself deeper. Cope with a situation like this in a manner that doesn't involve an internet connection!
- If you don't like the content a person is posting, simply and quietly unfriend them or block them. Don't make a spectacle of the situation.

TIPS TO NOT GETTING SCAMMED

We live in a world filled with people who want what you have.
Protect yourself!

Remember these tips to help keep you and the things you've worked for from being taken:

It's a SCAM!

- The IRS will *NEVER* call or email. They will only communicate through postal mail. Yes, I know this is a repeat, but it's important!
- Never open suspicious emails/links, especially from people or businesses you do not know. Scammers will text, email, contact through social media, and call people with award offers, deals, etc.
- Only make online purchases that are secure. Look at the site URL on the address bar; you want to see "HTTPS" and a lock icon.
- If you are unsure of the company, look them up on the Better Business Bureau site to ensure it is a legitimate business.
  ◊ BBB.org
- Be careful when dealing with people you do not know, try to never meet somebody at their house, and never go alone! *MEET IN A PUBLIC LOCATION WITH PEOPLE AROUND!*
- Do not share personal, identifiable information with anybody over the phone, email, or social media.

◊ Information such as bank account, personal financial information, Social Security number, birth date, etc.

- If it sounds too good to be true, it probably is. People may contact you with all of these fantastic offers and deals you can "only take advantage of if you act fast." *It's probably a scam!*
- Monitor your credit card and bank account info closely. If you see unknown charges, call the bank or creditor immediately to freeze your accounts.
  - ◊ Try to only sign up for new accounts that offer free fraud protection.

Call the Federal Trade Commission (FTC) to report scams.

- Phone #: 877-382-4357
- Site: usa.gov/where-report-scams

HERE'S A TIP... DON'T FORGET TO TIP

Don't be a jerk; tip service industry workers what they deserve, no matter what!

You never know what is going on in another person's life. Personally, I couldn't imagine working in the service industry where I would be expected to plaster on a fake smile and positive attitude, especially if my income depended on it!

If you find yourself being helped by someone who is clearly struggling with something, consider that showing them kindness can put a more positive spin on their day. Maybe there's a serious reason for their "poor" service that day, and receiving a nice tip and friendly conversation gives them some much-needed positivity in their life.

A GUIDELINE OF TIP-WORTHY SERVICES AND APPROPRIATE TIPPING AMOUNTS:

- **Dine-in food/drink service**: Tip at least 20%.
- **Delivery food/drink service:** Tip at least one dollar for every mile the delivery driver has to travel.
- **Self-care services (hair, nails, massages, facials, etc.):** Tip at least 15% to 20%.
- **Pet grooming:** Tip at least 15% to 20%.
- **Tattoos & piercings:** Tip at least 20%.
- **Uber, Lyft, or other personal transportation services:** Tip at least $2 to $5 for short trips, 15% to 20% for longer ones.
- **Parking attendant/valet services/bellhops:** Minimum of $2.
- **Bathroom attendants:** Minimum of $1 if you use any products or services offered.
- **Hotel employees:** Tips vary anywhere from $1 to $10 depending on services such as turndown/housekeeping, help with luggage, local activity recommendations.

TIPS FOR CALCULATING TIPS:

- Convert the percent to a decimal and then multiply your bill total by that number.
    - ◊ 10% = 0.1
    - ◊ 15% = 0.15
    - ◊ 20% = 0.2
    - ◊ 25% = 0.25
    - ◊ 30% = 0.3

◊ If your bill is $22.30, multiply that by 0.1 to get $2.23 for your 10% tip.

- You can also easily determine 10% of a total by moving the decimal one place to the left for the total cost.

  ◊ 10% of $75.00 is $7.50

    + If you are tipping 20%, then you simply double the amount.

HEALTHY COMMUNICATION

It is okay to agree to disagree with others; just do so with openness and kindness!

This is a topic I really wanted to address, though I struggled with where it fit within the framework of this book. Initially, I was going to add it to the "Treat Yo-Self" chapter, but after further thought — and by thought, I mean mildly obsessing — I decided it was best suited for this chapter.

FIRST, WHAT IS HEALTHY COMMUNICATION?

Healthy communication is the ability to have a conversation with others regarding topics you may not see eye to eye on. The conversation is carried on without using any type of negative language that will hurt people's feelings. Conversations in those negative tones significantly increase the likelihood of the conversation escalating into an argument.

To truly have a healthy conversation, all parties need to be honest and open to understanding everyone's point of view. If something is said that you may not fully understand, you should be able to feel comfortable asking questions to clarify that person's speaking point.

When you can have a conversation with a person on a topic that you have vastly different opinions on and walk away feeling light and happy, that right there is healthy communication!

Agreeing to disagree is going to happen, and it is up to the person speaking their mind to do so in a kind, unaggressive manner. Let me tell you, it makes all the difference in the world, and you may even learn some new things!

It is safe to say that everyone has likely experienced both the positive and negative effects words can have on others and yourself. Trust me, I have been on all ends of this spectrum. My fast-talking tendencies, coupled with my domineering opinions, get the best of me at times in my personal and professional lives.

I have damaged relationships with people who meant the world to me. I have alienated myself from others. And I have marred my reputation.

I have also used my words to uplift people, make them laugh and smile when they need it the most, help them see their worth, repair their self-esteem, and many other great things.

Let me tell you, out of the two options above, choosing kindness has *ALWAYS* left me feeling good about myself and the person I want people to see me as being. Every. Single. Time.

I never want my words to be the "last straw" that causes a person to decide to take their pain out through harmful actions to themselves or others. Always remember that you never know a person's entire life story and what factors were at play when they made the choices they did. This aspect of life is full of trial and error and lessons to learn and grow from if you choose to listen.

Healthy communication is crucial for both you and the parties you communicate with. We live in a world where people are super-quick to take offense to anything and everything a person might say... or type. "Computer crusaders" hiding in the comfort of their safe homes can be absolutely savage to others!

Here are some easy-to-follow bullet points to think about and do with what you will. Enjoy!

THE GOLDEN RULE:

Treat others as you would
want to be treated.

So simple. So solid. So often
broken.

- When meeting someone new, introduce yourself, make eye contact, and offer a firm handshake. It is respectful and a great way to make an excellent first impression on that person.
  ◊ You may have to substitute a different action in place of the handshake depending on the times. I have been writing this book amid a pandemic, when nobody is shaking hands anymore. I find that a friendly wave does the trick nicely.

- You will *never* know the full extent of a person's life and what they've been through to make them who they are today. Listen. Maybe you will learn something when you hear it from others' points of view. Maybe you can teach something too.

- Remember, the only person who can truly change you is you. If you decide to be negative and tear people down, prepare yourself for the consequences when you look around one day and see that nobody truly has your back.

- Opinions are like eyebrows: (almost) everyone has them, and they can present themselves in all kinds of ways. Just because you aren't fond of somebody's "brow game" doesn't mean you have to point it out and tell them all about it!

- If you are talking with someone who has different thoughts from what you do, ask them to explain their thought process instead of jumping down that person's throat. Have an honest, intellectual conversation and learn from one another.

- Before you tear down a person for saying or doing something you disagree with, take a step back and ask yourself these questions:
  ◊ Is this person physically or mentally harming anyone?

- ◊ Does their chosen way of living and expressing themselves negatively affect you in any way? Does it affect you positively?
- ◊ Do you know every single last detail about this person and why they act and think the way they do?
- ◊ More specifically, do you know what is going on in that person's life at this moment that could have an impact on their current mindset?
- ◊ What will you gain by telling that person they are wrong?
- ◊ How could your words impact that person?
- ◊ How could your words affect the way people see you? How do you want to be seen by others?
- ◊ Can you say with confidence that you are perfect and have done no wrong in your lifetime? No? Okay, why do you think you have the right to tell a person they're wrong?
- If you ever need a refresher course on how to be a kind, civil human being, revisit some children's shows from your past. Take the wise advice of an eggplant-colored reptile or some other brightly colored optimistic creature of your choosing!

Okay, this isn't a tip as much as a tiny rant. One thing I will NEVER understand is the kind of person who feels the need to put energy into spreading hate to others. The people who put time and money into creating elaborate signs and such and then stand on the street to tell people they probably don't even know how terrible they are. Like, what?!? What goes through a person's mind when they do that?

E. Z. TIP:

"This is such a great sign... it is totally going to change a person's fundamental beliefs and lifestyle choices!"

Not likely, pal. Leave happy people alone and put your energy into something that makes *you* happy and doesn't negatively affect others!

Frankly, I feel bad for those people, and I wonder what types of horrors they may have lived through to become that kind of person. I genuinely hope those people realize the errors in their ways and make an effort to evolve into better, more accepting versions of themselves. Being kind, if you ask me, is much easier and more gratifying.

Please don't get my words twisted, though. Not everyone holding signs on the streets and yelling are self-absorbed, energy-draining loons. I think people coming together to gather peacefully and unite against issues truly and negatively impacting people is a beautiful thing. It can show unity and passion and hopefully open somebody's eyes to something occurring in their community that they were previously unaware of.

THESE OLD-TIMEY THINGS CALLED MANNERS

Good manners and good people will carry you to a level of happiness that money can't buy!

Okay, young'ns, bear with me here. While we live in a time where technological advancements are ever-evolving, rendering many aspects of the "olden days" unnecessary, some things should carry on through generations. Those things are called *manners*. Here are some timeless manner tips to help you live your best and most respectful adulting lives:

- **Say PLEASE and THANK YOU:** A super-easy and polite way to let a person know you appreciate their time and effort!

- **Punctuality:** While being fashionably late in social settings is more acceptable, when it comes to professional engagements, tardiness is portrayed as being rude and disrespectful of others' time. If you say you are going to be at a certain place at a certain time, do it.
  - ◊ Life happens, and sometimes you may be forced to run late. If that is the case, make sure those affected are aware of your delay.

◊ If you choose to be a person who is chronically late, you are essentially telling people that you are not a person of your word. Be prepared to deal with the negative consequences that can come with this lifestyle choice.

◊ See **Appendix G** to learn how to read an analog clock to help you polish your punctuality skills!

- *HANDWRITTEN* **thank you notes:** When someone gives you a thoughtful gift, taking the time to write out and mail a card lets the person know you are grateful for them and the time and money they put into giving you that present.

  ◊ The keyword here is *handwritten*. No texts, social media posts, or emails; just good old-fashioned pen-to-paper writing and snail mail stamps. Not to mention, it's fun to receive positive letters in the mail and not just all bills!

- **Listen to others:** This is pretty straightforward, yet it can be a struggle for some. When a person is talking to you, listen to them and let them know you are *actually* paying attention.

  ◊ Active listening skills include eye contact and reacting appropriately to the tone of the conversation.

    + For example, Do NOT smile widely at a person telling you about their pet that passed away!

  ◊ Phone down, eyes up!

- **Compliment people:** It is so easy to compliment a person and be kind. Telling someone something as simple as "I love that shirt you are wearing" or "Your hair looks great" can really brighten a person's day. Never forget, kindness is contagious!

E. Z. & FRIENDS' TIPS FOR SMART ADULTING POP QUIZ!

Who doesn't love a pop quiz? Especially one where there are no wrong answers?!

Read each question and really take the time to ponder the answers — not how you *THINK* you should answer, but how you *WANT* to answer! Use the blank space below to write down your answers or anything you'd like. It is your book, after all!

E. Z. TIP:

To make this book personal to your life, write down your answers in the area provided and leave yourself some space to revamp your responses as you experience the different twists and turns of your adulting journey.

QUIZ QUESTIONS

Holy smokes, you finished the book! Let's wrap it up!

1. What topics piqued your interest the most?
2. What topics overwhelmed you to one degree or another?
3. How can you research these topics further to best educate yourself and ease any anxieties you may feel?

Use this space to start planning out your journey
to adulting happiness!

_____

_____

_____

_____

_____

_____

_____

_____

_____

_____

_____

_____

_____

_____

EPILOGUE

Well, that is all I've got for you for now. If this book is a hit, I have enough ideas swirling around this brain of mine to whip out an entire series chock-full of riveting, gritty content!

You are an awesome person who's capable of getting whatever you want out of this life if you're not afraid to work hard for it. One of my all-time favorite sayings and something I live by myself is, "You get out what you put in." There is truly no better feeling than achieving the goals that you have worked so hard to do. Make sure you are always taking pride in the things you are doing with your life.

You will make mistakes... probably lots of mistakes, but don't dwell on them. Shake it off, learn from it, and move on. It's called growth, and you should never stop doing it. For education is the key to eradicating one's ignorance. Never be afraid to admit you need help, and never feel bad about making choices that you feel are right. Okay, I am now annoying myself with the overabundance of motivational jargon. I'll stop now.

Whoa. You did it. You made it through the whole book! Or maybe you just skimmed it. Either way, if you are reading this sentence, you must have read something in the book, so good job!

If I was able to teach you something in this book, then I consider you to be an honorary student of mine. When it comes to my students, I try to help in any way that I can, and I am extending that offer to you as the owner of this book.

If you have any questions, comments, concerns, tips, ideas, comical anecdotes, anything, feel free to contact me through the form available on my site. Now get out there and slay it!

EZGRACEAUTHOR.COM

APPENDICES

APPENDIX A.
CREATE YOUR OWN BUDGET!

(Fill this out using a pencil so you can erase and update it as needed.)

_____'s Budget			
Total Monthly Income (After Taxes): $			
Paydays:			
Monthly Expense:	_Payment Date Due:_	_Amount Due:_	_Income Balance_
		$	$
		$	$
		$	$
		$	$
		$	$
		$	$
		$	$
		Bill Total: $	**Leftover Funds:** $
Yearly Expenses:	_Payment Due Date:_	_Amount Due:_	
		$	
		$	
		$	
		$	
Total Yearly Expenses to Budget For: $			

APPENDIX B.

GOOD JOB, NOW MAKE AN EMERGENCY FUND BUDGET!

(Fill this out using a pencil so you can erase and update it as needed.)

Emergency Budget Example				
Expense	Normal Amount	Emergency Budget Amount	Amount Saved	Notes
	Total:	Total:	Total:	

APPENDIX C.
PRACTICAL MATH CONVERSIONS!

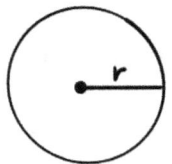 $$y(x) = 8\left(\frac{6 \cdot 4 + 3}{7 \cdot 6 - 3}\right)^2$$

I know math is not the most fun, especially the complex, unrealistic math that has likely been shoved down your throat your entire life. Don't worry; I'm not here to teach you about *that* kind of math. The following are common conversions you will *actually* use throughout your life. Read them, familiarize yourself with them, and then revisit this appendix anytime you need a refresher!

Common weight unit conversions:
- 1 kilogram (kg) = 2.2 pounds (lb)
- 1 gram (g) = 1000 milligrams (mg)
- 1 kilogram (kg) = 1000 grams (g)
- 1 ounce (oz) = 28 grams (g)
- 1 pound (lb) = 16 ounces (oz)

Common liquid unit conversions:
- 1 tablespoon (Tbsp or T) = 3 teaspoons (tsp or t)
- 1 cup (c) = 16 tablespoons (T) = 8 fluid ounces (fl oz)
- 1 pint (pt) = 2 cups (c)
- 1 quart (qt) = 2 pints (pt)
- 1 quart (qt) = 100 milliliters (mL)
- 1 gallon (gal) = 4 quarts (qt)
- 1 fluid ounce (fl oz) = 30 milliliters (mL)

- 1 milliliter (mL) = 1 cubic centimeter (cc)

Common linear measurement conversions:
- 1 foot (ft) = 12 inches (in)
- 1 inch (in) = 2.54 centimeters (cm)
- 1 inch (in) = 0.0254 meters (m)
- 1 foot (ft) = 0.3048 meters (m)
- 1 yard (yd) = 3 feet (ft)
- 1 meter (m) = 1.094 yards (yd)
- 1 kilometer (km) = 1000 meters (m) = 0.621 miles (mi)
- 1 mile (mi) = 1.609 kilometers (km)
- 1 mile (mi) = 1760 yards (yd) = 5280 feet (ft)

Temperature conversions:
- Celsius (C) to Fahrenheit (F): C = (F − 32) x 0.5556
- Fahrenheit (F) to Celsius (C): F = (C x 1.8) − 32
- REMEMBER: Always solve the problem inside the parentheses FIRST!

Converting fractions, decimals, and percentages:
- To convert a fraction to a decimal, you just divide the numerator (bottom number) by the denominator (top number). (EX: ¼ = 1 ÷ 4 = 0.25)
- To convert a decimal to a percentage, multiply the decimal by 100 OR move the decimal place over two spaces to the RIGHT. (EX: 0.75 x 100 = 75%)

APPENDIX D.

THE ALPHABET... IN CURSIVE!

These squiggly, weird letters are called cursive! The cursive alphabet and writing in cursive was something that everyone was taught in elementary school once upon a time. It's a lost art form cut from many required curriculums. It is something I feel everyone should have at least some basic knowledge of, as many folks in older generations still use it often. Your official adulting signature should be in a cursive format as well. Study up!

APPENDIX E.
MENTAL HEALTH CHECKUP:
KEEP TRACK OF YOUR BLESSINGS!

Life can get hard sometimes, really hard. It may even feel suffocating at times, making it hard to remember all the great things you have to be grateful for in your life.

Answer these questions, and when you are feeling gloomy, come back to this page and reflect upon your answers. Allow these answers to remind you how blessed you are and how much you have to live for.

1. What is the one place you would describe as being your "happy place"? A place that you feel safe in, where your worries begin to melt away? Describe that place below in enough detail that it makes you think of this place even when you aren't there.

_____

_____

_____

_____

_____

_____

_____

2. With each new season comes new activities and things to look forward to. What are the things you love about each season, whether it be activities, food, holidays, anything?

◇ Winter:

_____

_____

_____

◇ Spring:

_____

_____

_____

◇ Summer:

_____

_____

_____

◇ Fall:

_____

_____

_____

_____

3. What are your "Bucket List" dreams? No matter how grand or small they may be, if it is something you hope to do in your life, then it is important to you, and that's all that matters.

_____

_____

_____

_____

_____

_____

_____

_____

4. Remember that one time you laughed so incredibly hard that you were crying and maybe even on the verge of peeing your pants? Describe that time below, and don't skip out on any comical details!

_____

_____

_____

_____

_____

_____

_____

5. What hobbies and activities do you most enjoy doing?

_____

_____

_____

_____

_____

_____

_____

6. Describe a time that somebody went out of their way to help you. Now describe a time when you went out of your way to help someone. How did these experiences make you feel?

_____

_____

_____

_____

_____

_____

_____

_____

_____

7. What goals have you set for yourself that you have already achieved? How did you feel when you accomplished those goals?

_____

_____

_____

_____

_____

_____

_____

_____

8. Describe your dream vacation. What can you do to turn this dream into a reality one day?

_____

_____

_____

_____

_____

_____

_____

_____

9. The five senses can be used to easily transport us back to times when we felt truly happy. Describe an experience connected with each sense, an experience that triggers happy, positive memories. (For example, the smell of a campfire reminds me of the time I spent in the country with my family growing up.)

◊ Smell:

_____

_____

_____

_____

_____

◊ Taste:

_____

_____

_____

_____

◊ Touch:

_____

_____

_____

_____

◊ Sight:

_____

_____

_____

_____

_____

◊ Sound:

_____

_____

_____

_____

_____

10. Sit there and really think about your future. What is it that YOU want out of YOUR life? What will leave you feeling complete, satisfied, and happy?

_____

_____

_____

_____

_____

_____

_____

APPENDIX F.
RÉSUMÉ EXAMPLES

Here are two examples of résumés: one good, one bad. Look over them both to see the differences, especially how important proper verbiage and grammar is. I suggest you highlight different aspects of each résumé to focus on points you like and mistakes you want to avoid.

GOOD Résumé Features	BAD Résumé Follies
Résumé green flags:	**Résumé red flags:**

• Information is legible and written with proper spelling, grammar, and punctuation.
  • There are *so many* grammar correction programs available. USE THEM!
• Use 10- to 12-point font, depending on how long your résumé is.
  • Keep it under two pages.
• Use a basic font, such as Times New Roman, Calibri, or Arial.
• Set one-inch borders.
• Leave space between each section.
• Use single or 1.15 line spacing.
• Include lists of both hard and soft skills.
  • **Soft skills:** These are skills you develop naturally over time, such as time management and positive communication.
  • **Hard skills:** These are skills gained through education, hands-on experience, and specific training, such as software or program expertise.
	• Not following application directions.
	  • Every application process is **NOT** going to be the same.
	• Using different sizes and styles of font.
	
	  • Does **this** look professional?
	
	• Any kind of pictures.
	• An unprofessional email address.
	• Submitting a résumé that is too simple, shows no hint of your personality, or appears copied or generic.
	• Including job experiences and skills that have nothing to do with the job you are applying for.
	• Listing job experiences that imply you hop from job to job.
	  • It can make you come off as unreliable and undedicated. More details are below.
	• Over-emphasizing information that isn't important, such as GPA and other educational details.

Use one of the following format orders, first to last, when assembling your résumé:	DO NOT present information out of order; follow the natural timeline.

• **Functional:** Contact information, résumé objective, skills, experience, and education.
  • Good for creative jobs that require a portfolio and jobs you may appear overqualified for.
• **Chronological:** Contact information, summary or objective, experience, education, skills, and additional information.
  • Good for entry-level positions, student academics, or applying for a job in the same industry as your current job.
• **Combination:** Contact information, skills summary, additional skills, experience, and education.
  • Good for experienced applicants wanting a specific job, if you have employment gaps and career path changes.
	• Make sure you are listing education, experience, certifications, etc., in order by date.
	• List in reverse-chronological order (most recent first).
	
	PLEASE NOTE: Be prepared to explain any large gaps between employment and education. Gaps are **NOT** an automatic deal breaker with a proper explanation.
	• Identify the gaps and state whether it was personal or professional **WITHOUT** oversharing.
	• Explain them in a manner that shows you gained experience during that time, despite the gaps.
	• Keep your explanation positive.
	• Format your résumé in a manner that best highlights your strengths, despite any gaps.

Creatively word information to show-case skills and show measurable data highlighting your successes.	AVOID using personal pronouns (I, me, we, our, etc.) and judiciously omit some articles (a, an, the)

• Use this format when presenting skills.
  1. Action verb
  2. Project or task completed
  3. Measurable data and results
 	
• **Example:** Proposed a solution to help increase young-adult success by collaborating with a book coach and a team of literary industry professionals to create and market a book that became a bestseller within six months.
	• Employers know the information is about you. This helps avoid repetitive, unnecessary language.
	• It takes up space that should be used to highlight your strengths.
	• Your résumé will include a lot of incomplete sentences, and that is fine!
	
	Easy hack:
	
	• Write out the sentence you want.
	  • I managed a team of three.
	• Then take out pronouns and select articles and recheck that it still makes sense.
	  • Managed team of three.

Make sure the résumé you are sending is tailored for that specific job.	AVOID presenting information in paragraph form, making it harder to follow, and pick out details that can make you shine above the other candidates.

• This type of customization shows your interest and your attention to detail.
• Make a basic résumé template to keep on file highlighting what areas to customize. Then you can make a new copy for each job and swap out the highlighted areas for the custom information.
  • Adding bright highlighting will safeguard you from mistakenly sending the wrong information.
	• Use the minimal amount of words possible to ensure you are still highlighting your strengths.
	  • Remember, be confident but NOT cocky!
	• Format using bullet points and/or distinct sections.

APPENDIX G.
HOW TO READ AN ANALOG CLOCK

This may seem like a silly thing to add or feel the need to learn, but "retro" trends come back in style all the time, and some things are just good to know in general. I joke with my students sometimes by pulling out an analog clock and seeing who can read it and tell me the time without looking at their phones. The number of young people who can read an analog clock is alarmingly small. You cannot learn what you are not taught, so here is your official lesson!

- Understand and remember what each "hand" says:
  - ◊ The short/small hand tells you what hour it is.
  - ◊ The long/big hand tells you the minute of the hour.
  - ◊ The thin, fast-moving hand tells you the second of the minute.
- Note that the numbers on the clock tell you both the hours and the minutes.
  - ◊ The 1–12 numbers tell you the hour.

◊ When reading the minutes, the 1–12 numbers will be multiplied by 5.

+ 1 = 5 minutes
+ 2 = 10 minutes
+ 3 = 15 minutes
+ 4 = 20 minutes
+ 5 = 25 minutes
+ 6 = 30 minutes
+ 7 = 35 minutes
+ 8 = 40 minutes
+ 9 = 45 minutes
+ 10 = 50 minutes
+ 11 = 55 minutes
+ 12 = 60 minutes, the top of the hour

◊ Most analog clocks will have four small, dashed lines between each number. Each dashed line counts for 1 minute.

• Time-reading lingo:

◊ **Quarter past:** 15 minutes past the hour; the long hand will be on the number 3.

◊ **Half past:** 30 minutes past the hour; the long hand will be on the number 6.

◊ **Quarter till:** 45 minutes past the hour, or 15 minutes until the next hour; the long hand will be on the 9.

STEPS FOR READING THE CLOCK:

- First read the number that the short hand is pointing to. This will tell you what hour it is.
- Next, read the number that the long hand is pointing to. This will tell you the minutes within the hour.
    - ◊ Remember to convert the number into the minutes by multiplying by five and accounting for any small minute dashes to have the correct time.
- Now, put both hand values together to get the time. Simple as that!

◊ The time on the clock pictured is 3:28.

APPENDIX H.
WEBSITE INFORMATION

INTRODUCTION

Google Safe Browsing Transparency Report
transparencyreport.google.com/safe-browsing/search
Pg xxiii

GIVE YOURSELF SOME CREDIT

United States Courts: Chapter 7 Bankruptcy Basics
uscourts.gov/services-forms/bankruptcy/bankruptcy-basics/chapter-7-bankruptcy-basics
Pg 43

United States Courts: Chapter 13 Bankruptcy Basics
uscourts.gov/services-forms/bankruptcy/bankruptcy-basics/chapter-13-bankruptcy-basics
Pg 43

United States Courts: Bankruptcy Basics
uscourts.gov/services-forms/bankruptcy/bankruptcy-basics
Pg 43

TAXES ARE TAXING

IRS
irs.gov
Pg 92

YOU DONT NEED TO BE PERFECT, JUST INSURED

HealthCare.gov
healthcare.gov
Pg 108

OBTAINING & MAINTAINING A SWEET RIDE

Buying a Vehicle: A Guide to Missouri Title and Registration PDF
dor.mo.gov/forms/5687.pdf
Pg 132

TREAT YO-SELF

National Alliance on Mental Illness (NAMI)
nami.org
Pg 201

SO YOU GRADUATED HIGH SCHOOL. WHAT NOW?

US Department of Education
ed.gov
Pg 230

Council for Higher Education Accreditation (CHEA)
chea.org
Pg 230

FAFSA
ed.gov/about/contacts/state/index.html
Pg 235

Rock the Vote
rockthevote.org
Pg 248

Vote.gov
vote.gov
Pg 248

E.Z. & FRIENDS' TIPS FOR SMART ADULTING

Better Business Bureau

bbb.org

Pg 271

Federal Trade Commission

usa.gov/where-report-scams

Pg 272

EPILOGUE

E.Z. Grace Author Site

ezgraceauthor.com

Pg 289

INSURANCE NIGHTMARE BONUS STORY
THE E. Z. EXPERIENCE

I was at home doing laundry when I heard an odd dripping sound, so I leaned over from my comfy couch nest to see my kitchen floor turning into a lake! Insert panic here!!! First step, turn OFF the water ASAP!

Thankfully, I caught it, stopped it, and dried it up in a record amount of time. After soaking up the water, I pulled my washer out of its cubby to see that a hose had popped off during the spin cycle. I kid you not when I say the amount of water that came through that little unassuming hose was both impressive and panic-attack-inducing!

Unfortunately, I didn't get the water dried up fast enough, and some ended up leaking into the unit below me. Water follows the path of least resistance, and when you live in a home that is above others, that path is going to be down.

I was able to step back from the situation and turn my brain back on after all the water was mopped up and the dripping had stopped in my neighbor's unit. The first thing I did was call the company that I have my homeowners insurance through. I had never had to claim anything on this insurance, ever, so while I didn't know what to do, I knew they would.

After speaking with my agent, I learned that the next thing I had to do was get ahold of my condo association to inquire exactly how this type of situation should be handled. Not all HOAs are the same. Just as my agent predicted, handling this type of incident was clearly spelled out in our homeowner's association bylaws.

Our bylaws clearly state: if the source of the leak is not deemed as negligent, then each unit owner is required to file a claim through *their* own policy if there was any damage to *their* unit. It makes sense: *you* pay for *your* insurance policy to cover *your* belongings. I understood it; my neighbors did not.

WHEN THINGS STARTED TO GET ROCKY...

Ultimately, this insurance clause is a major annoyance for all involved and can quickly turn ugly when one party refuses to follow the given chain of command. I'll be the first to admit, I completely understand why my neighbors were upset. The water came from my unit, so why wouldn't I claim it on my insurance? Fortunately (for me), I did not have to claim it because both my HOA and my insurance company deemed the leak to be an accident, with no negligence on my part.

At the end of the day, it was an ACCIDENT, and that is exactly the reason we have insurance!

While trying my best to resolve this situation smoothly, I quickly learned it was really a lose-lose situation for all involved, me especially. My neighbors *refused* to listen to the communication from our condo association and my insurance agent explaining that this was standard procedure. They also *refused* to give me the name of their insurance company or accept the steps they were being told to follow.

My leak. My fault. My problem (and money). That was their stance, and they were not wavering on it, regardless of the facts. This stance took things to a very awkward, uncomfortable level. Quick!

Submitting this claim would likely result in their insurance premium raising, and they quickly made the argument of how unfair that was. Again, I'll admit it seems rather backward. I already felt awful that this had happened, and now trying to explain why they had to submit a claim through their insurance, not mine, made me feel even worse. Their refusing to listen made me feel very frustrated.

Should I insist they go through their insurance as the association policy states, or should I try and get a company to come out and assess the damage and just pay out of pocket? One answer is following the clear-cut protocol that was put in place long before this incident, but the other keeps the peace between neighbors. I put my mental health through a whole lot trying to figure out which path to take, putting me in quite the moral dilemma.

My neighbors decided to ignore the protocol and contacted a water remediation company to give them a quote on the damage. They texted, telling me they were quoted for up to $4,000 in repair costs by this company. I about stroked out, as they expected me to pay this cost out of pocket! After hearing their quote, I told them point blank, "I do not have that kind of money at all," and that we needed to proceed through our insurance as we were told to. Again, *this* is why people have insurance, right?!

Yet again, they refused to accept that, and it did not take long for the neighbors to start threatening legal action.

COMMUNICATION FRUSTRATIONS!

When it comes down to resolving a tension-laced situation, how you choose to communicate and handle yourself can have a HUGE influence on the conclusion. THINK BEFORE YOU SPEAK (OR TYPE)!

The following is a synopsis of the communication breakdowns from this problem.

- The chosen communication route my neighbor preferred to stick to was texting.
  - ◊ First, allow me to point out that texting about a matter like this was not the smartest tactic.
  - ◊ Texting about anything that could cause tension or strife is just silly. Don't do it if you don't have to!
  - ◊ Trying to portray any type of feeling in a text message is likely to be misconstrued, potentially making things worse (which it definitely did in this case; there's no misconstruing that!).
- ALWAYS keep this in mind: Any type of text message or email can be used as documentation if the matter ends up going to court.
  - ◊ It is hard to fight against clear documentation; your words can come back to bite you.
- After I was sent one last message threatening a lawsuit along with a bunch of screenshots with obscure information that was randomly highlighted (all in their favor, of course), I asked to speak with them in person.
  - ◊ I will admit, many of my friends warned me against this, but I can be stubborn, too, once my mind is made up! Ultimately, I chose this next action for personal reasons. My home is my

safe place, and I will do everything in my power to avoid having petty problems ruin that for me.

◊ While I can't say the conversation was productive, as neither of us were budging on our stance, it was obvious that neither of us were intentionally trying to "screw over" the other, which was a great sign!

◊ I came into the conversation open-minded and with a calm demeanor, which was a critical component for keeping the positivity alive. Otherwise, being told repeatedly that it's all my fault and I should shell out thousands of dollars to pay for this damage could've turned ugly and counterproductive... FAST!

• Keep this communication guidance in mind BEFORE you take the same steps I did!

◊ Coming into a situation such as this, hot and looking for a fight is only going to end badly — far worse than how it would end if you based your actions off strict facts and not feelings.

• If you do not fully trust yourself to keep your cool, then this is an action you should avoid.

◊ Personally, I am proud of myself for handling this in the matter I did, but admittedly, had this happened in my early 20s, I probably wouldn't have kept my cool so well.

◊ There is nothing embarrassing about admitting that you cannot come into a conflict such as this cool, calm, and collected. Actually, you should really be proud of yourself for knowing yourself well enough to choose the resolution route that works best for you.

NOT SO GRAND FINALE!

I wish I could say things resolved smoothly from there, but that wasn't the case. I truly came into this wanting to do everything to keep my neighbors from getting angry at me, potentially threatening my safe-place vibes. However, after speaking with my insurance company, the HOA, and a kind friend with a sibling who is a lawyer, I made the decision to stand my ground and insist that we settle this matter through insurance.

I spent a couple of hours carefully crafting a well-informed email, complete with sites explaining why it would be beneficial for them to go through insurance as well.

Had I let them convince me to pay out of pocket for a professional, and mold was in fact found, my next step would be ensuring that my small water leak was the source. I spoke with enough people in the construction/mold remediation industries to feel fairly confident that this water event would not produce mold.

The neighbors counterargued the fact that they had just bought the condo a couple of years ago and it was completely renovated — which it had been; I had seen a lot of it being done as I went about life.

However, and this is a BIG "however," in the state of Missouri, when a potential buyer has a property inspected that they are interested in, that home inspector will not automatically do any sort of mold testing. They *will* look for signs of water damage and mold, and if found, ask how you'd like to proceed.

What this means is that while their unit was remodeled, that doesn't mean it was done properly. The contractors could have torn out the drywall, found mold, decided they did not want to shell out thousands of dollars to have it fixed, and proceed to just slap up fresh drywall and paint over it.

No mold evidence, no need for an inspector to suggest further testing. Hence, this was the reason I would insist everything was done to find out if the mold was growing for weeks or years. Choosing to keep insurance out of this situation would be a gamble on both of our parts.

Had it been discovered mold was there long before this incident, I would require the neighbors to pay me back for the diagnostic fees, which would have been between $300 to $500 or more. AND *they* would be responsible for having the mold fixed, which would likely be several thousand dollars! If this scenario played out like this and the process was being completed through their insurance policy, they would save a ton of money.

I was proud of my research and response, confidently thinking they would understand and finally realize why I was adamantly pressing that we go the route we were told to go. I will admit that when I strongly suggested this route before learning the information I gathered, it made me feel a bit like a jerk, as the water was from my unit. What can you do, though, when that is the clear policy and protocol? I wasn't going to put myself in a ton of debt to appease people who by this point were being incredibly rude and threatening.

The response I received from the neighbors was not at all what I had hoped. My facts were shut down instantly and replaced with a string of nonsense. They described their version of the event and why they refused to follow the chain of command.

What was sent to me was different bits and pieces of our text and in-person conversations that were randomly spliced together and placed on a different timeline, which, of course, ended up sounding as if I was negligent and fully at blame. Not to mention all the immature, petty comments sprinkled in there too.

My blood pressure shot through the roof after reading that! It took nearly every ounce of self-control I had to not fire back a defensive response. Instead, I blocked their number and sent all of our communications to my insurance agent to ensure they were getting the full story and I was covering myself.

I spent the next several eerily quiet days filled with anxiety, just waiting for a legal aid to serve me with papers. As their last message made it clear, they would be taking this to court. I was more than confident that they had no case at all, but that wouldn't make the process any less stressful. I learned long ago that putting in the extra work to go the kinder route was always worth it in the end.

I waited. And waited. In the end, I never heard again from the neighbors, a lawyer, or their insurance. I can't help but believe they were trying to scam me all along, and I called their bluff by insisting we go through insurance. I'm sure it will eventually all work out, and while I don't see myself weaving friendship bracelets with them any time soon, I hope they will be mature about it all so we can avoid any majorly negative repercussions.

TAKEAWAY TIME!

First things first, if you find yourself in a sticky situation like this, PAY ATTENTION! Look at all the details and ensure you are actively listening to everything the other party is saying, as well as your insurance and any other governing parties responsible for resolving the issue.

Keep in mind that just because you receive communication that sounds intimidating or threatening, that does not make it right. FACT CHECK. In the end, it's not the person who is the bigger bully that wins, it is the person following the proper procedure. People will often talk a big game to intimidate the other party and try to force a win in their corner. When this happens, stay strong and follow your gut!

For example, my neighbor was sending me screenshots of different information she had found, making sure to highlight all the information that worked in her favor. Had I only read the highlighted text, I may have questioned if she was actually correct and change the way I handled things. However, I took the time to read the *whole* thing, especially taking note of the terms "flat" and "neighbour" being used. It didn't take a rocket scientist to quickly discover that she was sending me legal information from the UK, not the country we reside in.

If you don't *actually* know what you are talking about, it can be fairly obvious to the other party. If they call you on your bluff, all you did was lose credibility and damage your reputation. Be aware of this fact BEFORE you hit the send button on that message!

Bear in mind that laws, systems, policies, outlooks, etc., can greatly differ from country to country. Make sure you are sending information that applies to not only the situation but where it is taking place. Also, remember that in the United States, laws and policies are not united. Before you send "scary" threatening text messages to somebody, make sure that information applies to not only the correct country, but the state, city, county, and homeowner's association as well.

Next takeaway: Putting your automatic trust in a company or business is not smart. It's best to learn this lesson quickly once you're immersed in your adulting experience. It can save you lots of time, stress, and money.

Just because a company has a fancy website and advertises itself as being bonded or insured, or any other verbiage used to attract customers, that does not mean that business is focused on the client's need over their financial gain. Use the information provided in this book on the best ways to research a company and gauge their credibility based on what you find or do not find.

These days, way too many businesses look for uneducated clientele to take advantage of. It is not very hard to tell whether a person has actual knowledge regarding the matter at hand. Some companies will pick up on this right away and recommend unneeded services to rack up a larger bill and make a bigger profit.

Coming off as naive and uninterested in that particular service can cost you A LOT of money. If you don't want to learn about it, bring someone who does — someone you trust.

I had a strong feeling that this was exactly what happened when the neighbors got the free quote from a company they had called, especially after they gave me the whole detailed story when we spoke in person...

Get this: they informed me that on his way out, the contractor slipped them his personal number and let them know that he would fix the "damage" as a side job for only $1,500 — which is a total RED FLAG!!!

That right there should have told them the kind of "professional" they were dealing with — the kind that steals money from their own employer's pocket. If his employers were to learn of this, I imagine he would be fired immediately.

Drum roll please... Here is the number one, ultimate takeaway here: Be kind. Be patient. Be tolerant. Do all of that, but still STAND YOUR GROUND! Don't let another person's words bully you into making a decision you are not 110% comfortable with.

While there is nothing wrong with confiding in adults you trust, make sure that it is not your *only* source of information. I am sure you are thinking, why would my confidants steer me in the wrong direction? That answer can be as simple as them never having dealt with this scenario themselves, causing them to seek out guidance from those *they* confide in.

Had this happened to me when I was in my early 20s, like my neighbors are, I honestly can say I would have handled it all in a similar fashion, especially in regard to thinking that everything I am told by those I trust and respect is automatically true.

A person's age has no direct correlation with their knowledge. Education is key.

It's situations like these that make me step back and chuckle to myself for a moment. Adulting can be exactly like the telephone game children play. Do you remember playing that game? It starts with the original person whispering a sentence in the ear of the person next to them, then they whisper the sentence to the person next to them, and so on, until it travels all the way around the circle. By the time it gets around the circle, it is skewed to the point of being unrecognizable and often nonsensical.

This situation felt all too similar to that childhood game. In fact, the whole point of the game in general is to show how easily a person's words can be twisted and misused. Unfortunately, adulting "telephone" can be much more frustrating and costly, so keep that in mind before you start spouting off information with no factual basis.

If you are ever caught up in a conflict with someone like this, make sure to push the pause button at times to take the steps you need to look out for your own well-being!

I am aware this tale is a lengthy one, but if you made it this far, you have gained knowledge that can potentially be of tremendous use to you down the line. Here's to hoping that I don't publish a second edition of this book where I have to edit this story and explain how much worse things turned out!

ACKNOWLEDGMENTS

Good gravy, pals, I wrote a book! It is real, it is new, and it is NOW! Assuming you are presently holding my book and reading this, of course.

The creation of this book was a labor of love, and it would not have been possible without the support and help from the fantastic folks I am lucky enough to surround myself with every day. Words truly cannot express how thankful I am for my people, but I am going to do my best!

To my parents, Barb & Dale, you've supported (most) of the crazy decisions I have made in my life, and I wouldn't be who I am today without you. Huge thanks to you, Dad, for utilizing your technical editing skills. To Mom, thank you for proofreading my first very rough draft. Oh, and many thanks for giving birth to me; I really appreciate that!

To my dear friend Rebecca, nothing says friendship like holding Rebecca book-brainstorming sessions in obscure, receptionless, earth-home Airbnbs. I would not have wanted to share that experience with anybody else. Scratch that, it's not a proper ladies trip without Marsha! I do some of my best thinking when I start the day with a McMarsha! Our trips are always unforgettable, to say the least, and the memories we have made will keep me laughing for a lifetime! I am forever grateful for our weirdo bond and the support and guidance you've given me over the years.

To my students, past, present, and future: if it were not for you, this book would not exist. You inspire me to want to continually evolve to be the best version of myself and to help others in need in any way I can and know how to. I hope this book helps people learn things about life and themselves, just like you have all taught me to do.

To Nick, for helping with the creation of my pen name, among the many other things you've done for me. You nailed it instantly, saving me a lot of time and unnecessary anxiety. You tend to do that a lot! I am grateful for the person you are, and I am lucky to have you in my life. Who knows what I would be calling myself if you hadn't come up with this beauty during one of our many long, random, rambling conversations? I appreciate those conversations and support more than you know!

To my Rutabaga Squad, Katie, Sarah, Jessica, Marcie, and Olivia, the most fabulous group of pals a gal could ask for! Your strength, optimism, realism, and humor have kept a smile on my face through the many times I struggled to stay positive, especially while I was living the cat lady pandemic life! I truly hope everyone is as lucky as I am to have friends who build each other up and support one another as we do. You pack of weirdos mean the world to me!

GUYS... I wrote a book! Aaaayyyyoooo!!!

To the most amazing group of coworkers a person could have! Never in a million years did I think I would end up teaching one day, much less loving it the way I do. I have my peers to thank for being awesome role models, an amazing support system to lean on, and the best hilarious comic relief when I need it most. I adore the little school community we have and the Book Club meetings we've shared. I would not be the teacher or human I am today without all of you!

ACKNOWLEDGMENTS

I need to give a HUGE shout-out to those who coached me through this journey and gave me the tools needed to take this project of mine to the next level. Andrew Doty, I am so happy I found you and Editwright. I cannot even fathom what my book would be without your guidance; working with you has been an absolute pleasure, and I hope we get to work together on another book in the future!

A big thank you to those with the experience that helped guide me and ensure my book would be published looking as amazing and polished as possible; AJ Jepperson, Dana Zwaska, Chrissy Holder, and Karen L. Tucker. I greatly appreciate the time you put in, as well as working so graciously with a first-time author and self-publisher. I especially want to thank Allison Janicki for coming in clutch and getting us back on track and to the finish line! You helped make this journey a positive one for me, and I hope to work on future projects with all of you as well!

To *everyone*! I could honestly write another book just thanking those who have played an integral part in both my life and the creation of this book. Whether you helped proofread, donated time or money, partook in my "focus group" questions, or offered kind words of advice or encouragement, I am grateful beyond measure for everything you have done to support me!

That's all for now, folks! Help me make this book a big seller so I can write another installment. I've already got ideas swirling around my mind, ready to go! HUZZAH!

ABOUT THE AUTHOR

An educator, advocate, and now, published author, E. Z. Grace holds three degrees and teaches high school juniors and seniors. E. Z. has been involved in the education system for essentially her entire life, and after hearing nonstop comments from students about feeling unprepared for life after graduation, E. Z. decided to write a book that would not only benefit her own students, but young adults all around the country.

When she isn't strapped into her spin bike with her laptop, fully immersed in writing, you will likely find E. Z. working with animal rescues and enjoying time at home with her own zoo of misfit animals. Born and raised in St. Louis, MO, E. Z. loves gooey butter cake, toasted ravioli, and Imo's Pizza!

READY TO BOSS UP AND TAKE ON THE WORLD?

If this book helped you, please help me by giving it a 5-star review online so others can start working toward the adulting journeys of their dreams too!

Do you have any questions, comments, or concerns that you would like to discuss? Perhaps some ideas for important adulting topics I may have missed? Or maybe you are also passionate about providing critically important information in an equitable fashion and have ideas for how we can make a real impact!

Whatever you've got on your mind, to you I say…
LET'S CHAT!

EZGuides@ezgraceauthor.com

EZGraceAuthor.com